D1199041

meylan

635.9
c.1
Elb

Fun with
GROWING ODD AND CURIOUS HOUSE PLANTS

VIRGINIE F. and GEORGE A. ELBERT

CROWN PUBLISHERS, INC., NEW YORK

TO
RICHARD AND BETTY KELLY
WHO'VE TRIED EVERYTHING

© 1975 by Virginie F. and George A. Elbert. All rights reserved. No part of this book may be reproduced or utilized in any form or by any means, electronic or mechanical, including photocopying, recording, or by any information storage and retrieval system, without permission in writing from the Publisher. Inquiries should be addressed to Crown Publishers, Inc., 419 Park Avenue South, New York, N.Y. 10016

Printed in the United States of America
Published simultaneously in Canada by
General Publishing Company Limited

Design: Deborah M. Daly

Library of Congress Cataloging in Publication Data

Elbert, Virginie.
    Fun with growing odd and curious house plants.

    Bibliography: p.
    Includes index.
    1. House plants.   I. Elbert, George, 1911-
joint author.   II. Title.
SB419.E44   635.9′65   75-17828
    ISBN 0-517-51653-5
    ISBN 0-517-51654-3 pbk.

CONTENTS

Acknowledgments

The authors are most grateful for assistance in securing
illustrations for this book from:

Mr. Thomas H. Everett of the New York Botanical Garden
Mr. Donald Richardson of Greentree
The Geo. W. Park Seed Company
Mr. Richard C. Peterson of the American Orchid Society

and from those splendid English photographers:
Mr. Bernard Alfieri
Miss Margaret Martin
Mr. Peter R. Chapman

Miss Elizabeth C. Hall, that greatest of horticultural librarians,
has been, as always, immensely helpful.

1 It's Fun To Be Different

Now that so many more plants can be grown indoors, people are discovering as never before, face to face as it were, how very extraordinary plants can be. As long as they were just slow-growing clusters of greenery that stood in the corner of a room and were dusted once in a while, they seemed very dull things indeed, good only as a sort of vegetable statuary—a static ornament to a room. To be sure, there have always been the bulb plants that blossom for a short time each year. And for the holidays and special occasions there were gift plants, splashes of color which lasted a couple of weeks, and, having collapsed, were tossed out with the refuse. Really handsome plants were grown only by enthusiastic amateurs, and continuous bloom was unknown. Only the indestructible plants survived in an apartment, and even most houses were no places for adventurous growing.

We might say that plants indoors had very little personality. In the home animal pets—our dogs and cats and lovebirds—were ever so much more interesting and responsive. And the thought never occurred to anyone but the most rabid fan that such dull things as plants could also impress us as having individuality and character. Of course we don't want to give the false impression that we consider the vegetable kingdom to be responsive to our thoughts and feelings, as some would have us believe. But we are now discovering, through a more intimate contact than ever before, that plants *do* respond to care, that they can offer us changes from day to day, and that among them are innumerable kinds that are not only beautiful but display idiosyncrasies which are funny, fascinating, and baffling. Depending on our tastes, there is an infinite number of peculiarities to attract us and, indeed, to satisfy the particular needs of any human being for qualities that suit his particular cast of mind or sense.

The greatest enemy of true enjoyment in growing is convention. No two people are completely alike and, if we sometimes act like a herd of sheep, that is not because there are no differences among us so much as our tendency to sublimate tastes and opinions in order to conform. When, in spring, you drive south of the Mason and Dixon line past innumerable plantings of the same red azaleas, it is not because everybody loves this one kind better than the many other choices available. It's more a demonstration of the power of convention. And if the suburban garden in the North is one unvarying planting of petunias, marigolds, and zinnias, the same is true. In both instances what is planted is proper and doesn't make a person stand out from his fellows, is safe and sure, and can't be criticized as a departure from normal practice.

Convention also rules our automatic responses to flowers. Nobody dares not *Love* flowers and saying so is quite enough. And we *Adore* roses because roses are Beautiful. Such reactions are as meaningless as they are universal and by no means express the innate attitude, which has as many nuances as there are people. In the same way we can afford to ignore most plants completely because no convention forces us to approve them or to interest ourselves in them. Even among plant lovers we find those who confine themselves to one specialty, although they are by no means professionals or experts, and close their minds to knowledge of any others.

Very general is the convention that flowers are beautiful—in principle. But, in order to be spared a glance or a phrase, they must be violently colored and preferably large. A big dahlia or moth orchid is more beautiful than a small one. Our real sensual and emotional reactions to any plant have far more to do with the qualities of our own sensibility than with a characteristic of the plant itself. Any aspect of nature can be beautiful to some and not to others. Beauty in fact is a very complex matter and, if we look into our own souls, instead of aping our neighbors, we find that we react in a very different way from others.

As we come to know plants better, we begin to relate our personal interests and feelings more closely to our choices. Bigness, symmetry, and bright color are no longer the only criteria. Even the visual appearance of a plant may not be of primary interest. As we have pointed out in our book *Fun with Growing Herbs Indoors*, people can like herbs, indeed develop the most intense attachment to them, because of their culinary uses, an interest in their medicinal values, an enthusiasm for their fragrances, a fascination with their supposed magical or mythical virtues, or for their historical associations. In the same way we can enjoy a plant because it suggests age, as with bonsai, or reflects the buffets of a rigorous environment like so many of our most curious plants.

The moment we drop our conventional attitudes toward plants a whole new range of interests develop. If *we* are curious we will discover how exciting and curious *they* can be. Once we have broken free of the fear of change and of the unknown, once we have the courage to try new plants, we become engaged in an entirely different kind of collecting and growing. Instead of being repelled by an unfamiliar plant we are attracted to it because of its potential of revealing a new aspect of plant growth or providing a novel pleasure. The field is realized as so diverse, so incredibly varied, that we can find types that conform to our individual needs and our innate desires.

The collection of plants described in this book and the information we have chosen to provide are meant not merely to introduce you to some unusual examples but to suggest the vastness of the plant world accessible to the indoor grower and to encourage you to venture forth on your own, following the thread of one or another of our leads. That is why we have chosen few monstrosities and have confined ourselves (with one exception) to plants that can be grown in the house and without special skill. These, we hope, will start you off to learn more about growing plants and their peculiarities, permitting you to cultivate the more esoteric ones and to discover the magnificent treasures that nature offers us.

Imitation and emulation in growing plants can be satisfactory, but the real fun starts when you choose and care for something different as the result of your own curiosity and your own inner relationship to plants.

2 Growing Indoors

THE NORMAL HOME

No, we are not going to get into home economics, home decoration as such, home repair, or the composition of the typical American family. But, taking plants as our starting point, there is something we can describe as a normal home environment. If we add a few exceptions you will be able to understand, allowing for the differences in your own home, just what we mean when we use a phrase like "normal house temperature" or "normal house humidity" or light. This is necessary because, though the plants we describe are partly different from the ones to which you are accustomed, they can all be grown in this normal home environment.

There are two major categories of indoor environments for plants—country home and city apartment. City is consistently more difficult than country growing because of aerial pollution, which is harmful to plants and cuts down on light. Although foliage is not much affected, many blooming plants that perform satisfactorily in a country house will not flower at all in the city.

TEMPERATURE

The average American home is maintained at a minimum temperature of 60° throughout the year. When it is cold outdoors, a spot close to a window will reach much lower temperatures. There are some who prefer a cooler home and, for this reason, can grow some plants others can't. For instance, orchids and Alpine plants do well in a cool cellar. But, since the majority of our house plants are of tropical origin, the loss in variety is greater than the gain.

Our normal summer temperatures are very high. On hot days the thermometer may register close to 100° F. Above 85° F the effect on plants may be as debilitating as on people. The ideal range is 65° to 75° for most of the exotics. Air-conditioned homes are usually maintained within it. The advantage of artificial cooling is considerable. The resulting reduction in humidity can be compensated by various means.

Because of our indoor temperature range, several categories of plants must be eliminated from consideration. Perennials requiring a winter freeze are impractical indoors unless you can winter them in the open. Bulbs, such as lilies, can be treated to a cold spell of six to eight weeks in the refrigerator to make them grow and bloom, but only experts are successful with them in the house. Cacti and succulents can tolerate cool temperatures and some require freezing conditions. The reason why some of these attractive plants will not bloom in the house may be the lack of a cold period—or shorter light days than are normal with us. If you choose the relatively warm-growing ones, you are much more likely to induce bloom indoors. On the other hand, some tropicals require really steamy conditions and are not for the average, rather dry, home. Annuals do well, but for a relatively short season. For many plants we do not yet know the exact conditions required to make them bloom indoors. Often we are familiar with conditions in their habitats but not the degree of change they will tolerate, if we are unable to duplicate them.

These problems and limitations may seem severe, but are considerably less so than those imposed by climate on your outdoor gardening choices.

HUMIDITY

Many of our tropical indoor plants prefer a humidity of 50 percent or higher summer and winter. Both air-conditioned and radiator-heated houses register very low humidity, usually below 30 percent. In summer the house is less humid with air conditioning than without it.

Either grow plants, of which we list several, that are indifferent to low humidity, or find some means to raise the moisture level of the air. Just placing a few plants in their pots over a bed of moist pebbles or plastic crate (see below) is not very effective, although better than nothing. A great many plants packed into a small room will raise the humidity considerably as long as they are kept well watered. But the only sure way is to install a room humidifier with a built-in humidistat. This instrument is not very accurate, but will keep the humidity within a workable range. Small models need constant refilling. Best are the 8-to-10-gallon stand-up types.

Plastic crate or "egg crate" is molded plastic sheeting, mostly used as a light diffuser in elevator ceilings, provided with openings which are square or hexagonal. The sheet is ½ inch thick, 2 feet wide, and 4 feet long and can be cut easily with a saw. We very much prefer it to using pebbles in trays as a support for pots because plastic crate is light and clean. Set the crate in the bottom of your trays and maintain a constant film of water. Lacking a humidifier, frequent mistings will help your plants.

NATURAL LIGHT

Natural light is the most difficult matter to assess. Nowadays in the North not many homes have sun porches, but those that do enjoy above-average lighting summer and winter. However, since the vast majority of homes lack this advantage we must use ordinary window light in the country and the city as our standard.

Windowsills in the country enjoy several hours of sunlight summer and winter from the three major exposures. But that, let us note, is very close to the panes. The angle of the sun in summer is more favorable to an eastern and western than to a southern exposure. At its zenith, the sun is too high to reach more than the front row of plants with a southern exposure, while the direct east and west rays reach farther into the room and for a longer period of time. In winter south is the best exposure, for then the sun does not rise so high and the plants enjoy longer hours of direct illumination, while toward the east and west the windowsill has direct sun for a relatively short period.

Formerly indoor gardening was overwhelmingly a spring-summer affair and the recommendation to place plants in east or west windows made sense. But now that we grow and bloom all year round, east and west are inferior to south. For, though a southern exposure receives shorter hours of light in summer (the angle is more vertical), in winter the light days are longer (light angle is more horizontal). When someone boasts how well he grows in an east or west window, find out at what time of year he has bloom on his plants. South, therefore, is the position we call normal for full sunlight on the windowsill and east and west for partial sunlight or partial shade.

Periods of cloudy weather cause unpredictable results in windowsill plantings. No matter how brightly the sun may shine for a long period, if cloudy days ensue at the wrong time for a plant, it will not bloom. The unreliability of continuous sunny days is one of the principal reasons why we have come to depend more on fluorescent lighting. When we speak of good or full sun we mean continuous sunlight in a southern exposure. Should the weather turn unfavorable for long periods, all bets are off.

We also bring to your attention the fact that modern houses and apartments are built with very little provision for plant space at windows. Bays are rare. Heating units are often situated just below the windows and make it difficult to grow anything in winter unless the heat is turned off. Under any circumstances the full sun space at a window is very small indeed. Consider the width of the window as the base of a triangle and draw the sides into the room at an angle of 45°. That is the area of usable sunlight. You will discover that it is very small. If your windows are double or triple you will find that toward the tip of the triangle the height of plants—because the windows themselves are wider than high—is reduced to zero before you have reached the tip of your flat triangle. The area therefore is wider than with a single window but not much deeper into the room. Outside of the triangular area only foliage plants can be grown and, even these, for only a limited distance.

Natural light in the city is at least 30 percent lower than in the country due to smog, buildings in the way, and dirt on the windows. Even some African violets require a fully sunny position in the city. Figure on only the front row of plants receiving enough light to be approximately equivalent to "partial sunlight." That is why city people who claim to have all the sunlight they need for their plants are almost invariably mistaken and, when one asks with what plants they are successful, we find out that they are just foliage plants which do not even require the amount of light they are being given.

We are so conditioned to summer gardening—closing down in September and suffering indoors through the winter with a few very adaptable plants—that it is difficult for us to become accustomed to the fact that winter blooming is now, due to artificial lighting, not only possible but especially desirable. For most of the population, which lives in urban or suburban conditions, summer flowers in the home are by no means a necessity. This is the time for vacations, weekends at lake or shore, and much more visiting. It is in winter that we need and always have needed plants, especially flowering ones. Now we can reverse the seasons and have them when they are most desirable. This development does not relate as closely to the contents of this book, which contain only a few of the plants which bloom particularly well in the house, as to indoor gardening in general. But it does suggest that the most desirable plants are not so much those which are active in summer as those which put on a display in winter. The new indoor gardening permits us not only to grow blooming plants in winter but supplies us with a respectable repertory of those that flower continuously through all the seasons.

FLUORESCENT LIGHT FOR MAINTENANCE AND BLOOM

The module we use throughout this book is a reflector fixture with two 20-watt, 24-inch fluorescent lamps—one Warm White and one Cool White. We have found this setup quite effective in maintaining and blooming plants the year round. Temperatures are maintained at over 60° F. The lights are left on fourteen to sixteen hours a day for most plants. In consideration of the shortage of energy and rising costs we have tried twelve hours and achieved almost equal results. The 40-watt, 48-inch lamps are more efficient, and four to eight such lamps set side by side with 4-to-6-inch spacing provide not only more garden space but even better results. We set the tops of the plants from 3 to 18 inches under the lamps, depending on type. This is a lot of leeway but only experience can teach you the best position, as conditions vary in every home. The most effective single lamp is the Verilux-TruBloom.

Attach or hang the fixtures under shelving, cabinets, or tables. Support them on wall brackets. Install them inside cabinets. If the under surface to which they are attached is painted white for reflection, ordinary strip fixtures without reflectors can be used. There are also a considerable number of manufactured light gardens on the market either as table models or tiered shelving.

An automatic timer is virtually a must. The principal source of heat in these fixtures, which are much cooler than incandescent lighting, is the ballast inside the metal box to which the lamp sockets are attached. Open the box, unscrew the ballast, extend the wires, and hang the ballast where it will not raise the temperature around the plants. All fluorescent fixtures should be grounded.

INCANDESCENT LIGHT

Incandescent lamps are so much less efficient than fluorescent tubes and produce so much heat that they cannot be used for blooming plants. Because of certain experiments carried on by the USDA in growth chambers, which showed that a combination of fluorescent and incandescent lamps was effective for seedlings, the impression has gotten around that this illumination is also useful to the average indoor grower. This is not the case, and artificial light is no longer in favor. Exaggerated claims have been made by some manufacturers for lamps of this type, but in practice these lamps are feasible only for the maintenance of foliage plants.

However, where we are interested only in keeping foliage plants alive and well, provided we can cut down on the heat emission, flood and spot incandescent light can be suitable. General Electric's Cool Beam and Sylvania's Cool-Lux are floodlights using a glass filter that reflects the heat rays so that they do not reach the plant. Because all the heat is thrown backward, ceramic sockets must be used. Otherwise these are ordinary bulbs possessing a spectrum quite adequate for plant growth. Set from one to three feet above foliage plants they do a good job. Lamps lacking the dichroic filter but promoted for their "growth spectrum" are not recommended. Major manufacturers have not pressed the sale of "cool" floods only because the public is careless and does not install the ceramic socket, which is available from any hardware store or electrical supply store. Without this precaution there can be accidents.

The so-called plant-lite floods are very inadequate and inferior to normal floodlights.

We have recommended Warm White and Cool White lamps in combination as the ones which are most economical and efficient. Growth lamps, such as Agro-Lite, Gro-Lux, and Naturescent vary in effectiveness and are more costly. Grow-Lux *Wide Spectrum,* a less expensive lamp, is in our opinion better than the others. But, if you want a lamp that is easier on the eyes, more natural in appearance than any of the others, producing compact plants, better leaf and flower color, and longer-lasting blooms, then Tru-Bloom, manufactured by Verilux, Inc., justifies its higher price. A recent addition to the list, this is a real breakthrough in plant-growth lighting.

To improve blooming in a window garden install fluorescent lighting and turn it on for six hours after sundown. Still better is to install a sensor which will, in addition, turn on the lights during cloudy periods.

Other lights than those recommended—often termed "growth lamps"—offer no advantage that we can see. Do not be misled by exaggerated claims or scientific gobbledegook. So-called High Output lamps are also a snare and a delusion. The addition of normal lamps to a set will be more effective. As for some of the new sources of illumination—metal halide and sodium lamps—which are enormously powerful, these have been created for other purposes and are not yet adapted to home use.

SOIL

The advantages of soilless mix have been too well demonstrated to be arguable anymore. The modern indoor gardener uses it exclusively. That doesn't mean that it is perfect, merely that it is at present the simplest and most successful soil for houseplants.

Garden and other outdoor soils dry out very fast in the house, require sterilizing, which is a messy business, and rarely provide the mechanical characteristics we need for tropical plants. The old, complex combinations of humus, leafmold, and sand are totally obsolete. The first thing we do when we acquire a plant in ordinary soil is to repot it in soilless mix. Almost invariably when left in the ordinary soil the plant degenerates after a short time indoors. Our warning against ordinary soils extends also to products called "potting soils" in variety stores and garden centers. And we cannot recommend any of the packaged soilless mixes for the reason that they use very finely divided material which becomes a mush in the pot, and they often contain fertilizer material harmful to our plants. It is so easy to prepare your own soilless mix that any other solution strikes us as a heavy risk to take with plants—for a very slight convenience.

Our mixes contain as primary components just three materials. Peat moss is the partly decayed residue of sphagnum moss, which grows in the bogs of cold climates. It is fibrous and water retentive. But Canadian sphagnum peat moss, not Michigan peat. Perlite is obsidian exploded at high temperatures. White, gritty, and granular, it aerates the soil and acts like an excellent quality sand. Vermiculite is mica that has been exploded by heat so that the thin crystals separate, forming accordionlike cubes. Although they absorb no water the innumerable crystals hold water by tension. It is a wonderful material by itself for rooting cuttings of plants. All three materials can be purchased in convenient-sized, plastic bags at variety stores, florists, nurseries, and garden centers.

Our mixes are made by stirring together the components in a dry state and then moistening before potting. Throughout the book the mixes will be labeled as below.

Rich Mix   3 cups peat moss
                  2 cups perlite
                  1 cup vermiculite
    This is the equivalent of a soil rich in humus.

Lean Mix   1 cup peat moss
                  1 cup perlite
                  1 cup vermiculite
      Plants accustomed to a "poor" soil prefer this mixture.

Cactus and
Succulent Mix   1 cup peat moss
                  2 cups perlite
                  2 cups vermiculite
      For desert plants.

Few of our houseplants prefer an acid soil, but those that do will be happy in these mixes. For most of the others we add lime in the form of chips, eggshells (crushed), or horticultural lime powder at the rate of two tablespoons to a quart. This will offset the natural acidity of the peat moss. Lime should not be added in regions where the water is "hard."

The orchid family requires special mixes that are available from orchid nurseries. There are two types, one for epiphytic (tree growing) and the other for terrestrial (ground plant) species.

FERTILIZER

Plants require nutrition, but this does not come from soil of a mineral consistency except through the action of weather, bacteria, and animals. Soil is also enriched in nature by decay of plants. In the house the soil we use is sterile. Therefore we must supply all the necessary nutriment to maintain a plant and make it grow.

The vital elements necessary to plant growth and bloom are nitrogen (nitrates), phosphorus (phosphates), and potassium (potash). Indoor growers need only small quantitites of these fertilizers in the form of soluble crystals or granules that are formulated, packaged, and sold everywhere that plants are marketed. The active elements of organic fertilizers of which, for the indoor grower, the most important is fish emulsion, are the same.

There are any number of brands of fertilizer on the market, all of which bear on their labels the content in percentages of these three elements. They are always listed in the same sequence as above. For instance, 30–10–10 on the label means that the fertilizer contains 30 percent nitrogen, 10 percent phosphorus, and 10 percent potassium. This is a typical *High Nitrogen* formula, which is the way we describe it in our cultural information. It is best for acid-loving plants and for fast foliage growth.

For many plants a *Balanced Formula* is best, such as 20–20–20 (or 10–10–10). This is an all-around safe type of formula. If you wish to encourage bud formation and flowering, switch to a formula high in phosphorus such as 5–10–5 or even higher in the phosphorus figure. This we call *High Phosphate* formula. African violet growers who want to keep their plants in constant bloom use such fertilizers regularly.

Some growers fertilize with each watering, while others prefer to do it once a week. Very few go to the trouble of controlling nutrition for each plant separately. Fortunately the easier way works very well. If you want to fertilize every day, it is advisable to dilute with ten times as much water as is indicated on the label of the package. For instance, if the label calls for one tablespoon of fertilizer to a gallon of water you will have to figure out one tenth of a tablespoon. In practice we find that this is equivalent to the amount you could pick up on the point of a knife—or a small pinch. If you fertilize only once a week, cut the labeled quantity to a quarter. That means one-half teaspoon to a gallon of water. Don't worry about this being too little. Once people start fertilizing at all, they generally overdo it rather than the opposite.

Although there are various organic fertilizers on the market, the only one which is generally used is fish emulsion. This is now deodorized for the squeamish. It is a liquid that should be used in the proportions mentioned above. An excellent fertilizer, it is somewhat on the acid side (high in nitrate). We don't like to use either chemical or fish emulsion fertilizer for too long, but prefer to alternate them from time to time. It seems to work very well. One reason may be that fish emulsion naturally contains some trace elements.

These trace elements are ones which plants require in minute quantities. Small as the intake may be it is absolutely necessary for some plants. When buying chemical fertilizers you will note that some contain trace elements. Those are the ones we prefer to use. In addition some plants—especially those that are acid lovers—need iron. This is available as iron chelate or under the brand name Sequestrene (Geigy). But there is usually enough iron in peat moss to suit your plants.

Cacti and succulents normally require not only less water but less fertilizer than other plants. Fertilize only when the plants are growing and don't use more than one tenth the concentration recommended on the label. Even the concentration of fish emulsion should be drastically reduced. Overfertilization will burn the roots.

Fertilizer should be added to moist, not dry, soil. Otherwise the solution comes into direct contact with the roots immediately. If a plant is very dry, moisten with plain water first, then give a second watering a few hours later with dissolved fertilizer.

WATER

The most difficult technique to master with plants is proper watering, and it is one that is acquired only with experience. It is that aspect of your care of a plant to which it reacts most rapidly and obviously, and for whose effects you must watch it most closely. Each kind of plant requires a certain amount of water at certain intervals and there is no rule that covers them all. However, there *are* some rules that are unchanging. Here they are.

1. Never use water colder than room temperature.

2. Use water from the warm water faucet. It is generally less loaded with chemical additives at the time it leaves the tap and you are less likely to draw the water cold.

3. Water a plant more when it is growing—putting out new leaves or branches. When it ceases growing, depending on the plant, you must either reduce waterings drastically or eliminate them altogether.

4. Water more in warm than in cool weather.

5. You can fill a saucer under a pot and let a plant absorb the moisture but never allow it to stand in the water for long, unless it has been well tested with this treatment.

6. Make sure that the soil in the pot is well packed. If it is loose in one part the water will run right through and both the rest of the soil and the roots may remain bone dry. After plants have been potted for a while, poke around in the soil to make sure that it is firm everywhere in the pot. Soilless mix has a particularly bad habit of settling and will produce gaps, after a period in the pot, that must be filled in with new soil.

Because plants dry out more in the house than in a greenhouse, they need more watering. Most will be happy if you can keep them evenly moist. Not all plants will tolerate even a day of drying out. Something to watch is the speed with which your plants absorb water. You will notice that some are much heavier drinkers than others.

There is no real difference between watering from the top or the bottom. We do prefer bottom watering because there is no risk of wetting axils of leaves, which have a tendency to rot. But the principle is the same. If you water from the top, see that the liquid runs through and then dump the excess in the saucer or tray. If you water from the bottom fill the saucers. Return in a half hour and throw out any excess water. Saucers that are dry may need a second filling.

Plastic crate (see p.10) acts like a wick when there is water in the tray. This may have the effect of keeping some plants too wet. If you find this to be so, provide them with saucers. On the other hand the crate does cut down on watering chores for all the plants that like constant moisture.

Wicking has its passionate adherents. There is the kind, consisting of fiberglass cord, which is poked up through the hole in the bottom of the pot and dangled into a water source. There are others that arch from an outside water source into the top of the pot. Again, plants that do not like much moisture or constant moisture may suffer, while others will flourish. If you raise a mixed collection of plants, you will find some that will not tolerate wicking.

VACATIONS

A serious problem arises when we leave our plants even for a weekend away from home, and this becomes a real headache if a lengthier vacation is in prospect. How can we protect our plants against dying of thirst during our absence?

Many troublesome and ineffective ways have been suggested for protecting plants during a period when they will receive no care. And no method is absolutely foolproof except a plant sitter who is knowledgeable and conscientious—an almost impossible paragon. Here is our formula.

Windowsill plants. Remove the plants from all but mild reflected light. Allow cacti and succulents to dry out in a coolish place. The foliage plants should all be wicked. There are several methods of wicking that are satisfactory. All they require is a large reservoir of water with leads to the different pots. The new method with the curved wick going from the water reservoir to the top of the pot is very convenient. If the plants are in trays supported by pebbles or plastic crate, fill the trays as much as possible—to just touch the bottoms of the pots. If you can cover the whole area with a plastic sheet you have double protection.

Fluorescent light gardens. Put the lights on a five-hour cycle. Fill the trays with water and cover the whole garden with a plastic sheet.

When you return you may not find all your plants reveling in this treatment, but at least most of them will survive. We rarely lose a plant this way.

POTS AND POTTING

Although the aesthetic appearance of clay pots is preferred by many, the plastic pot has largely superseded them for indoor growing. We use plastic for two reasons—they retain moisture better and take up less space. Young plants, such as vegetative rootings, are usually potted up in 1½-inch plastic pots, then moved to 2- or 2½-inchers and wind up in those with a diameter of 4 inches. Most indoor blooming plants need nothing larger, and by this means we can grow many plants in a small space. Of course, when it is desirable to grow a specimen plant or a good-sized shrub or small tree, much larger pots are needed, and then we may need clay pots for their weight and rigidity, and wooden tubs.

Plants with hanging branches must be either supported in some way in their pots so that there is room for the stems or hung in pots with attached saucers or baskets. Wire baskets must be lined with sheet moss and then packed with soil. We hang pots by chain, macramé weavings, or wire.

There are many details of potting techniques that we have no space here to discuss. Generally speaking, plants should be handled by their leaves or branches when young and never by their stems until these are rigid. In potting, the soil should reach just to the meeting place of stem and root. Packing must be inward from the wall of the pot, never pressing down hard around the stem. Lately we have been using a potting stick in emulation of orchid fanciers. A potting stick is nothing more than a dowel with a blunt broad point. This is jabbed into the soil along the wall of the pot, and the soil is then levered toward the center of the pot and the open spaces filled in. In this way less damage is done to the roots of the plant.

In transplanting from one pot to another, we first knock the ball of root and earth out of the smaller pot by rapping its edge against the side of a table or bowl, usually in a moist state. Soil is poured in the bottom of the larger pot and the plant root and soil ball tested for height in relation to the edge of the new pot. When this has been established, soil is filled in around the plant and tamped down and in with the potting stick.

Newly potted plants often need some protection for a few days. Cover with a clear plastic bag and gradually lift as the plant hardens off.

Modern indoor growing has eliminated drainage in the bottom of pots except for orchids. There are many reasons why drainage was needed years ago, for instance to protect the plants against excessive moisture during moist cold periods. But, with our evenly heated homes and low humidity, it has become entirely superfluous and an extravagant waste of space. Without drainage you can leave a plant in a pot for a much longer period of growth.

MULTIPLYING YOUR PLANTS

The modern indoor grower is discovering what fun it is to multiply plants. Before the artificial light gardening era started, the number of plants one could grow in the home was very limited, and there was very little reason to try to multiply those one had. But now that we can have gardens anywhere indoors that space allows, we can indulge in this enjoyable activity.

Plants do not last forever and many are rather short-lived. There is also the fact that many of them reach maturity and maximum beauty and thereafter become less and less attractive. If we are to have our plants looking their best, new ones must be coming along all the time, and it is far more satisfactory to grow vegetatively from plants we have chosen and enjoy them than to go forth each time and acquire new ones by purchase.

Whenever we buy a plant at a nursery, we take a cutting as soon as we have brought it home. The change of environment is often lethal to the mother plant but our cutting will survive. Even when the original plant does grow well, we find that our cutting, because it has been grown entirely indoors, does even better.

A special joy of gardening is the sharing with friends. If we have a particularly fine plant, there is always someone happy to have a duplicate.

Certain plants must always be grown from seed, but with many others this is only necessary the first time. Thereafter we can propagate by cuttings. Seed often does not come true from the parent plant, while vegetative cuttings always do. If you have a color you like or a plant that has particularly fine characteristics, the way to multiply it is by means of rooted cuttings. It is only recently that we have become aware that many of our annual plants, once we have plants from seed, can be continued much more rapidly and effectively by the vegetative method. In this way you can have a constant succession of plants in perfect condition with little effort and within a very small space.

SEEDING

Indoors we need very few seeds for sowing. Commercial packets usually contain a number sufficient for garden use, which involves rowing or massing. Therefore, do not figure, for each variety of seed, on more than a half dozen at most to a planting unless you really want to propagate a lot of them for friends. Good seed will provide better than 80 percent germination.

Use a plastic container just large enough for your needs. A plastic cream cup may serve for a couple of tiny seeds. A half dozen may be planted in plastic old-fashioned glasses and a plastic shoe box will hold ten or more rows with different varieties of seed.

Fill the container (which should not have a drainage hole) with an inch to an inch and a half of moist Lean Mix. Sow small seed on top and larger seed pressed to its own depth into the soil.

It will be helpful to the survival of your seedlings if you acquire milled sphagnum moss, available in small plastic bags, and cover the soil with the thinnest of layers in the dried state. It will moisten when the container is covered.

Cover the container with a plastic lid or a piece of transparent sheeting.

Set the container in a warm place ranging in temperature from 72° to 80° F. The top of a fluorescent light unit is ideal—just over the ballast. The box should have good reflected light but never receive direct sunlight.

Germination time varies from a few days to months. Be patient and leave your box alone. If it remains closed the moisture will be sufficient for a long time and the less disturbance the better.

When seedlings appear, gradually lift the edge of the plastic to harden them off. A period of a couple of weeks is required. The soil can be misted if it starts to dry out on the surface. Once the seedlings are able to stand normal air they can be transplanted to pots without damage.

Don't forget to label the seed row or pot. It is remarkably easy to forget what has been planted.

This method is suitable for most of our small houseplant seeds. However, there are many tropical plants that require special treatment, which varies according to the type. Some need soaking, others a filing of the shell to speed moistening. Certain seeds need removal from their shells entirely. We often simply toss large tropical seeds with hard shells into a plastic bag with moist moss and place them over bottom heat. Left to themselves they will germinate under these conditions. Seed catalogs sometimes give instructions for the treatment of these special seeds. John Brudy's (see source list) contains excellent directions.

In most instances, once you have plants from seed, further propagation can be carried on by the much more important and satisfactory (indoors) vegetative method.

PROPAGATING VEGETATIVELY

Most houseplants will produce roots and new top growth if sections of stem or branch with leaves are cut free and planted under suitable conditions, thus creating a new plant that is exactly like the parent.

When a plant has grown large enough to be trimmed, in other words has several branches, sever one or more branches three or more nodes below the growing tip. A node is a place where leaves are attached.

Use any plastic container that is high enough to accommodate one or more cuttings. Fill the bottom with moist, not wet, vermiculite, remove the lowest pair of leaves, cutting them close to but not flush with the stem, and plant this lowest node in the vermiculite. Cover the box with a transparent lid or a piece of clear plastic and set in reflected light of a window or under artificial light in a temperature of 70° to 80°. In a couple of weeks open the box and give a tug on the cutting. If it resists strongly, it is rooted. Should you, by mistake, pull out the cutting before it is properly rooted, stuff it back into the vermiculite and try again later. When a ½ inch or more of root is showing, pot the cutting in soilless mix, cover for a couple of days until it has convalesced from the change, and then put it out on the windowsill or the shelf of your light garden. That is all there is to it.

Dipping the tip of the cutting into Hormodin or Rootone powder before planting may encourage root formation.

Not all cuttings require covering during the rooting process. *Lantana, Crossandra*, and others will do just as well in an open box. But you will have to learn which is best by experience. The tenderer plants do need the box.

The leaves of some plants, mostly gesneriads and succulents, will root in moist vermiculite in the open. It is only necessary to bury part of the leaf in the soil. Sections of stem of the arum family, enclosed in a plastic bag with moist moss, will sprout and root with time. Plants with stolons (runners) are a special case. The stolons with their leafy tips can be cut off and treated like any other cutting. But they can also be pinned down with hairpins, while still attached to the mother plant, into soil of small pots. When the tips have rooted you can cut the umbilical cord.

Thus, according to the habit of the plant, there are these and several other ways of inducing pieces of a plant to root and grow.

TERRARIUM CULTURE

Some of the best of the new tropical plants for the house either need terrarium conditions or do better in them. Naturally these are the smaller plants. Terrariums are not only beautiful, if well planted, but are safe to leave untouched during vacations away from home and safe against marauding cats or children. You will find detailed instructions and designs in our book *Fun with Terrarium Gardening* (Crown). Here we can give you only a few details about culture.

We use Lean Mix in our terrariums and moisten it just enough to be evident. When pressed in the hand, there should not be enough moisture to glue the mass together. The mix is laid over a layer of perlite or lime chips. Plants are left in their pots and buried in the areas where soil is sufficiently deep to hide them. Stones are used to prop up the soil and help hide the pots.

The modern terrarium contains blooming as well as foliage plants. *Sinningia pusilla* is a typical example of an everblooming terrarium plant. A terrarium must be covered by a transparent sheet of glass or plastic. This can be opened with discretion on hot humid days or if there is evidence—heavy water drops on the glass—of excess moisture.

No terrarium should ever be set in sunlight. Indirect light is the most it can stand. Artificial light from fluorescent lamps is very superior. A 2-tube, 24-watt fixture can be suspended 3 or 4 inches over the top of the terrarium and left on fourteen to sixteen hours a day.

For terrariums, glass is very superior to plastic, which invariably deteriorates with time.

In tank terrariums, plants can be arranged in their pots very attractively without any foundation soil. Cactus and succulent gardens, which are kept quite dry, look magnificent with rocks and a sand top dressing.

3 Naming Plants

A long time ago botanists decided that Latin was the best language for naming plants. That avoided two horrible prospects—that each language use its own vocabulary for plants or that all the countries become involved in an interminable and insoluble squabble as to whose language would be used exclusively. The system has worked very well and has prevented the confusion arising from common names. If you think that common names are an easier method of communication consider first the different languages involved—the common names are different in each one—and the confusion created by the use of the same common names for several very different plants. The trouble people have learning Latin names is largely imaginary. Many of our common names are either very similar to or identical with the Latin or Greek ones and we never give it a thought. Rhododendron, Campanula, Azalea, Verbena, Acacia, Chrysanthemum, Lantana, and Camellia are no more difficult than other correct names for plants. They are merely more familiar. Learning the common name of an unfamiliar plant is no easier than learning the Latin one. And it is only the Latin one that identifies your plant beyond question or doubt.

For as long as they have been published, seed and plant catalogs have used common names—each in their own language—which are either traditional or invented on the spot as a sales gimmick. A typical device is to invent a new name for a plant that has a well-known common one. Readers of the catalog assume that they are dealing with a novelty—only to discover too late that they've been took. Even experienced plantsmen are confused by some of these catalog names.

In naming plants for our cultural section we have used the same freedom and invented descriptive names for these odd and curious plants. Some are well-known common names, hallowed by use in florist shops and nurseries. Others are pure inventions on our part, admittedly to whet your interest.

Underneath the heading we have listed the Latin name and have also used it in our text. In this way we hope to succeed in keeping the timorous from taking flight and at the same time lead them gently into proper terminology. In short, some of our names, appropriate as they may be, are a spoof.

In our text we mention the families of plants. These are the larger groupings to which plants belong. The proper name of the plant lists first the genus and then the species. This is a bit like writing our names. Elbert could be our genus, George and Virginie our species, and we are Americans—that is our family. We only mention the family or nation when we compare the origins of the Smiths, the Rousseaus, or the Schmidts. The members of a plant family show basic resemblances, those of a genus are alike in greater detail, and the individual species differentiate still finer peculiarities. For instance *Stapelia gigantea* belongs to the milkweed family or *Asclepiadaceae,* named for the genus *Asclepias* to which most of our common milkweeds belong. *Stapelia* is a genus with the same kinds of pods, seeds, and certain other details as all other milkweed family plants. Only these are succulents with columnar stems and no leaves. *Gigantea* describes the supersize of the particular flower of the species. So it is with all other plants.

How wild the common name business could become is indicated by the use of names for cultivated or hybridized plants. They are given all kinds of names, just like racehorses—everything from Baby Doll to President Carnot—and only a real expert can learn them or tell them apart. If we used common names for the original wild plants we would be completely lost. So learn your Latin names.

Aechmea fasciata—*the most beautiful and popular bromeliad. This variety is streaked with darker horizontal barrings. The strong stem and solid look of the flower cluster suggest that it is long lasting, which it is.*

4 Tropical Sundae Flowers

AECHMEA FASCIATA

Of all the "air plants" this one has enjoyed the most consistent popularity for the longest time. Like the Cattleya orchid it attracted attention as soon as it was introduced into cultivation in 1826. Today it is so much in demand that commercial nurserymen have found it advantageous to grow as fast as they can in preference to many other handsome species and cultivars, so that one might say that it has driven these others out of the market.

Aechmea fasciata combines all the virtues of an ideal gift plant. Its flowering is altogether unusual and spectacular; the inflorescence lasts for months; the grey green barred foliage is beautiful at any time; and it needs little attention in the house. As a steady houseplant, it has the disadvantage of large size and the difficulty of causing it to bloom again.

This wonderful plant comes from southern Brazil where it attaches itself to trees. On page 154 we discuss the bromeliads, which are air plants and are nourished by means of a coating of scales on the leaves. Aechmea, although possessing these scales, is of the "vase" type that collects water in its center. So it's a kind that needs more filling than spraying and will survive as long as its reservoir is supplied with water. Some bromeliads have so large a vessel that they are the habitat of tiny plants, insects, and frogs. The more the merrier, for these supply additional nourishment to the plant.

The perfect symmetry is one of the attractions of aechmea. The leaves, 3 inches wide and up to 18 inches long, are packed in a tight rosette always leaving a funnel in the very middle. The leaves are grey and in many cultivars beautifully barred horizontally or longitudinally. Out of the center grows a thick stalk which tops off in a bouquet of pink bracts dotted with purple flowers. The effect is truly like some artistic and exotic sundae, so different from other flowerings and so appetizing that one might almost be tempted to try to eat it. The leatheriness of the leaves and bracts and their hard, short spines would discourage any trial.

When the bloom finally fades, after several dustings, aechmea produces suckers from the base and the mother plant dies off. The suckers, when they have acquired a bit of root, must be cut loose, dug up, and potted separately in any organic, preferably fibrous acid mix. Getting these to reach flowering size again, as in a greenhouse, is not that easy. The plants need plenty of moderate sunlight or a very favored position under the lights. That isn't easy. There are too many cloudy days in the North, and light gardens usually don't have sufficient room for so large a plant. But, if you keep the vase filled with the mildest of acid (high nitrogen) fertilizer solutions, mist regularly, and provide the necessary amount of light, you too can bloom aechmea.

If size is a real drawback look around for other aechmeas of which there are many which are both beautiful and fairly compact.

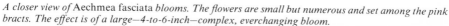

A closer view of Aechmea fasciata *blooms. The flowers are small but numerous and set among the pink bracts. The effect is of a large—4-to-6-inch—complex, everchanging bloom.*

Aloe vera—*a number of the aloes look very much alike when young and share the same "miraculous" healing qualities. They make attractive, fast-growing, trouble-free pot plants.*

5 The Incredible Aloe
ALOE VERA

Aloe vera (or *barbadensis)* has become something of a legend. It's just an ordinary-looking aloe, which means that it has fleshy tubular speckled green leaves that, in nature, grow to 3 feet in length. By that time the stem is 3 feet high and puts up a tall stalk which bears numerous pendent, yellow, bell flowers. Early on, the natives of the West Indian islands discovered that the juice was a handy purgative when taken internally and effective externally in relieving minor burns and insect bites.

When queen bee jelly (remember it?) lost its spell as the cosmetic guaranteed to rejuvenate the aging epidermis, our *Aloe vera* took its place. Many were the testimonials to the miraculous action of Mother Nature's gift to mankind. Oceans of lotions were produced with the power to banish sunburn, turn your wrinkles into peach bloom skin, remove all blemishes, and grow hair on the baldest pate. If you have a plant and faith in the doctrine, put your aloe in the blender, reduce it to a mush, and smear it on anything that is bothering you. Otherwise just grow it as a pleasant and easy houseplant.

Young specimens can be bought small and cheap. Never mind; they grow faster than any other succulent around. Any kind of soil seems satisfactory, but we use Lean Mix and place them in a sunny window or anywhere under lights. We water regularly for they have no tendency to rot unless the temperature gets down below 55°. In no time they are producing quantities of offspring from the base. Separate the young ones with some root and pot them up. Or you can move the whole cluster to larger and larger pots with most interesting effects of aloe thickets. Aloes being quick-growing plants, you can get plenty of action. Fertilizer is hardly necessary but 20–20–20 solution every couple of months is beneficial. Flowering in the home is rare. You will need a big pot and the best sunny exposure to accomplish it.

Other aloes are equally or more attractive. A particularly beautiful form is *Aloe variegata* which has white spots arranged in stripes, a more compact growth than *Aloe vera*, and more propensity to bloom with bright red flowers. *Aloe aristata, humilis, brevifolia, ciliaris, ferox*, and *mitriformis* are among the many choices. At a nursery you can pick out the colors and shapes you like. The culture is the same for all. It is not true that they should be watered less in winter, unless the house is especially cool. Under modern home conditions aloes will continue to produce healthy growth the year round.

The true, true upright growth and handsome inflorescence of Aloe vera. *Photo courtesy of Thomas H. Everett.*

The beautifully spotted Aloe variegata *is a compact and trouble-free pot plant.*

This *is how big your "miniature" pineapple will have to grow to provide fruit for the table. The superminiatures are inedible, though sufficiently odd looking.*

⑥ Grow Your Own Pineapple?
ANANAS COMOSUS

Buy one of those really big "sugarloaf" pineapples in the market. Cut off the tuft of leaves at the top along with an inch of fruit. Eat the rest of the pineapple. Take the top piece and scrape out the juicy fruit, leaving the center core and the skin. Allow it to dry for three days, then plant up to the base of the leaves in moist Lean Mix with lime. Set the plant in a bright window, mist the leaves every day, and give the soil a little water. In a few weeks it should start to grow from the center, losing some of the outer leaves in the process. From then on during the summer months spray and water regularly with 30–10–10 fertilizer and always pour some water into the center. Treat pretty much the same in winter except cut down a bit on the watering. Temperature should stay above 60° F. As the plant gets bigger, it will have to moved to larger pots.

Soon you will have a plant with a spread of 3 feet and the beginnings of some pretty sharp spines. The color is generally grey green. In three years it will be 5 feet across and the spines will be truly ferocious. You will have a devil of a time watering your pineapple, since proximity becomes more and more dangerous. Along about the fifth year your plant will still have no pineapple, and you decide to give up on that part and either accept your spiny monster as it is or throw it out. No pineapple either way.

Well, try again. This time buy one of the small pineapples, treat the top in the same way, and nurse it along. In a few months this kind will be quite green and will be ringed by a fine bunch of pups. As these spread, move the whole business to a larger pot. Real fun. Now you have a small forest of pineapple plants with their leaves all entangled and beginning to flop out of the pot. Very interesting. But no pineapple.

We once knew a lady who triumphantly told us that she had raised a pineapple and, when it was ripe, invited all her friends over to have a chunk of homegrown. We believe her. But as more than one have said, one swallow doesn't make a summer. Your chance of fruiting a pineapple plant is about a zillion to one. The various commercial types of pineapple plant are among the less attractive members of the bromeliad family. If you grow for foliage any number of bromeliads are beautifully colored and striped, and the best cultivated varieties are easy to bloom and stay colorful for months. So why grow a pineapple at all?

All right—you do want that fruit which is, after all, unique. The only reasonable solution is to buy a plant already in fruit. Southern nurseries offer very compact plants with a central spike and a little pineapple that, if you put it in the brightest sunshine and water and fertilize as we have suggested, will grow to a respectable if not commercial size. It will even be sweet and edible. Some of the plants have variegated leaves and are relatively spineless.

After fruiting, these plants will produce pups, which can be separated from the mother plant when they are 8 inches high and possess some roots of their own. You can then try to grow several pineapple plants at once. But don't plan on a pineapple festival. The odds continue to be pretty steep.

Lately we have seen some particularly handsome variegated pineapple plants. These had pink, white, and green in longitudinal stripes. Breeding has made this ugly duckling into a swan among bromeliads. They're not great for fruit but truly pretty.

A decorative pineapple. Even the leaves coming out of the top of the fruit are variegated. The spines are real and will keep your animal pets at bay.

Darwin's orchid, Angraecum sesquipedale. *The spurs containing the nectar are unbelievably long. The flower is huge and waxy—up to 7 inches across.*

7 Darwin's Orchid

ANGRAECUM SESQUIPEDALE

The most curious anecdote in all the long history of orchid collecting, growing, and research is that of Darwin's orchid. From December 1831 to October 1836 the young naturalist was sailing around the world on HMS *Beagle* as part of a team sent out to study all aspects of nature in little-known areas of the globe. From this voyage he came back to write his famous diary and, eventually, *Origin of Species,* which was published in 1859.

Among the places visited by the expedition was Madagascar. Earlier in the voyage Darwin had noticed the curious pollination mechanisms of orchids. On the island he was immediately intrigued by a large, waxy white orchid with a nectar spur almost a foot long. Good scientists don't just notice; they ask questions. For Darwin the first question was: Why did the flower have such a long spur? The answer—because its pollinating visitor must possess an equally long proboscis. The next question was: Which insect fits the description? With no opportunity to watch the flower for a long enough period, he guessed that it was a nocturnal moth. But local inquiries elicited no information about such an insect.

When Darwin reported his theory, the reaction was that he must be kidding and that such absurdities were inconceivable. Proof of the correctness of his deduction came twenty years later when a moth was collected in Madagascar that had the required specifications. With a wingspread of only 5½ inches, its proboscis was a foot long. In honor of the occasion the insect received the resounding title *Xanthopan morganii praedicta*. That raises the question why not *darwinii?*

After the publication of *Origin* Darwin, in the process of defending his theories, issued a little book called *The Various Contrivances by which British and Foreign Orchids are Fertilized by Insects*. It is an exquisite little work, written with great clarity and charm. If you have any curiosity about the sex life of the sexiest plants, you should read it. The subject has been updated in *Orchid Flowers* by van der Pijl and Dodson, University of Miami Press. That contains even more spectacular information and pictures.

The name of Darwin's orchid is *Angraecum sesquipedale*. Because it is as beautiful as its history is curious, it is a popular plant and is offered by many orchid nurseries. Also it is among the most handsome of the warm growing orchids which are adapted to windowsill growing. The plant produces two to four fragrant white flowers 7 inches across.

Angraecums are vinelike orchids with a single strong thick stem and opposite, strap-shaped leaves. It grows best attached to tree fern poles or

The huge flower of Angraecum sesquipedale *with the spur that astonished Darwin and led to his prediction of an equally extraordinary moth.* Photo courtesy of Thomas H. Everett.

slabs. Mature plants require 6-to-12-inch pots. Pot in standard orchid epiphytic mix consisting of firbark, redwood chips, tree fern, and so on. It is best to buy the mixture from an orchid nursery since the average houseplant grower will find it a nuisance to gather the ingredients himself.

This is a large plant and should be placed in a sunny window. It likes high humidity and constant moisture. A morning and evening spraying will do the trick. Fertilize once a week with 30–10–10 formula.

Bloom takes place in the middle of winter, between December and February. The flowers are long lasting. Angraecum develops roots at the upper nodes of the stem. Cut off the stem just below and pot the section with its root. By this means you keep the plant within bounds and have an interesting gift for friends.

Those of you who are concerned about growing such a large plant will find the smaller species of angraecum a delight. And some of these have relatively long spurs to remind you of their relative. Jones & Scully (see source list) offer *A. chloranthum, eburneum, eichlerianum, magdalenae, philippinense, and viguieri. Magdalenae* is a beautiful miniature but not cheap. All these plants are warm growers, which are relatively easy indoors. In fact the angraecums are to be especially recommended for growing under lights.

Darwin's moth—wingspread 5½ inches, proboscis 12 inches or more. The only insect in the world which can pollinate An-graecum sesquipedale, *the Madagascan orchid.*

The unique asparagus fern—Asparagus meyeri with its "foxtail" stems.

 Foxtail Asparagus
ASPARAGUS MEYERI

We who live in the city know very well where things come from and how they are made. Milk and cream are products of a factory and come in plastic-coated cardboard containers. Bacon is a form of sliced fat packed in plastic. Bread is made of flour which is some sort of chemical. Naturally asparagus, such as we eat boiled with Hollandaise Sauce or plain butter and lemon, is a mature vegetable like a carrot and just grows that way.

Down in south New Jersey you can see fields, from train or car, usually in June, of tall whippy canes bearing feathery foliage and quite large red berries. If you ask the farmers, they will tell you that's asparagus. Some jokers, those farmers.

Of course that isn't the asparagus you eat. That's the asparagus plant in fruit—botanically *Asparagus officinalis* var. *altilis,* a European seashore plant, something of a weed, which farmers like to grow for some reason.

Asparagus plumosus, the asparagus fern, is another matter entirely, since we buy it not in the vegetable store but the florist. The other asparagus with the bigger needles is *A. sprengeri* which nobody has

33

given a common name. They're both from South Africa. At this point we suddenly find out that there are a number of other ornamental asparaguses and will start to notice especially *Asparagus meyeri*, which we call the foxtail asparagus, because that is what it looks like. This one, too, is from South Africa. For a while every florist shop seemed to have them. But it turns out that the seed crops of these unusual asparaguses are unreliable, and this fact, combined with an enormous increase in houseplant buying, which cleaned up every *Asparagus meyeri* plant in sight, has created a temporary scarcity which may prove to be not so temporary after all. Still, seed is offered by a few firms and, if you are willing to grow from scratch, you can have this most unusual foliage plant after all.

It is unlikely that there are any plants of such large size with leaves as fine as the asparaguses. Asparagus fern leaves grow by the thousands horizontally along the side branches and are, individually, almost too narrow to be seen. When the foliage dies it disintegrates into brown dust which makes it one of the messiest of plants. Other relatives have somewhat larger leaves arranged in various ways. But *A. meyeri* does something which is very special. The short branches grow like wheel spokes all around the arching stems from one end to the other. Each branch carries a whorl of needles. Since branches and needles are uniform in length they form a solid tube of greenery except where they become shorter toward the tips of the stems. Full-grown plants present a very strange appearance for the fat tails arch out on all sides, for up to eighteen inches from the centers.

Although most people like the mature plants, we like the young ones better because at that time the stems are erect, the branches shorter, and the effect is less heavy. Somehow a full-grown plant looks ungainly, like an animal whose tail is too heavy for its body—a fat-tailed sheep for instance.

By all means acquire a young plant rather than grow from seed. Seed takes thirty days to germinate which is a bit long for most people, and growth at first is slow. In potting use Rich Mix with lime. Place the plant in reflected light or 12 inches below the fluorescent lamps. Fleshy oval tubers are produced, which lie close to the surface of the soil. These are, of course, for water storage in periods of drought. If you don't moisten *A. meyeri* sufficiently, it will die down, but will recover, even after months, if watering is resumed. In spite of this trait most of us prefer to water this fern constantly, allowing it to dry out a bit only during cool periods. It will tolerate 50° or less but a minimum of 60° is preferable. Fertilize with a balanced solution or fish emulsion.

If the fern is given good sunlight and the stems reach maturity, you may get flowers, which will be small, white, and six-petaled like the lily family to which the asparagus belongs. The flowering takes place all along and around the greenery. The fruits are round, about the size of small peas, and red. Cherish and dry the fruits, extract the seeds, and distribute them among your friends.

A young bird's-nest fern. New leaves develop from the center.

The Bird's-Nest Fern

ASPLENIUM NIDUS-AVIS

It is not our choice that two ferns follow each other but rather the fact that they both belong to the same genus—*Asplenium*. This, too, is a curious relationship for they could hardly look less alike. This will get you used to the idea that recognizing plants of the same genus by their "lookalikeness" often doesn't work.

The tricky thing about this fern is that its leaves are perfectly simple, long spoon shapes, with a midrib and nary a frill. Furthermore it has a black-haired central button of tissue around which the leaves emerge and unroll forming a complete circle, several layers deep in mature plants. In nature the leaves may grow to 4 feet, and sometimes in botanical gardens you will see them in big tubs. In the house we usually grow them smaller and are satisfied eventually with a fine specimen in a little tub. *Asplenium nidus-avis,* our subject, can be bought quite small—just 3 or 4 inches high. But it will soon flesh out and produce 10-to-12-inch leaves which have a delightfully cool look. Although its appearance is so exotic, it is an easy plant to grow and should be a lot more popular than it is.

Since growth is moderately rapid, repotting must take place after six months (a 4-incher) in Rich Mix packed rather loosely. Keep the plant moist at all times and in good reflected light or under fluorescent illumination if you have room. The bird's-nest fern prefers high humidity but won't show any more damage to leaves from normal living room dryness than a bit of browning of the edges and some crimping. Misting will keep this under control. Fertilize with 30-10-10 solution or fish emulsion once a month. Being a semitropical fern, the temperature should be maintained above 55° at all times. Its progressive growth will eventually lead to a tub, by which time it will have become something of a show plant. Since it is very beautiful and the leaves are quite erect so that it doesn't take up very much room, you will certainly not have the heart to dispose of it. You may end up showing your splendid monster with great pride and giving your other ferns away to friends to make room for it.

The way you usually see Beaucarnea recurvata—*as a juvenile. The pony tail is a sign of adult status.* Photo courtesy of Thomas H. Everett.

10 The Pony Tail Plant

BEAUCARNEA RECURVATA

At garden centers and nurseries, where they are fairly common, you can buy the so-called pony tail plant, *Beaucarnea recurvata*. It is a pretty plant with a little domed fat swollen trunk surmounted by an arching spray of long narrow leaves. It really does deserve its name at this age, which is juvenile. When it is old enough to vote it might be called the hippy plant.

As far as we are concerned, patience plant would do. We bought a young one fifteen years ago. Since then it has been sitting well back from our front window and has grown—but, oh, so slowly. Now it is a yard high and an amusing sort of monster. The trunk, now 6 inches across and 5 inches high, looks like a partly buried bulb covered with dusty elephant hide. Out of its center rises the thick branchless straight stalk—a yard high. In the last foot it explodes into long narrow trailing leaves that extend right down to the bottom of the 12-inch pot in which it lives.

When we bought our plant in Fort Myers, Florida, it was labeled Nolina. It is probably the usual *Beaucarnea recurvata* of the shops, which as a young plant is virtually indistinguishable from the several Nolina species. These plants come from the Southwest and Baja California, where they share the wretched growing conditions of the boojum tree. Some other specimens we saw at the time were being offered in huge tubs and had trunks 2 feet across and stems 10 feet high. We would have dearly loved to have one but transportation presented a slight problem—something like a piano. We suppose that out West these big specimens are common and don't raise an eyebrow. But here in the East our plant creates a sensation wherever it is displayed. People think it is a rare species instead of the plant they themselves may have at home—only much older.

Beaucarnea belongs to the lily family, which may strike you as somewhat odd. But its resemblance to that section of the family which includes the dracaenas and yuccas is pretty obvious. We have a yucca at home which we dug up as a young plant off the beach of Sanibel Island (Florida). It is the Spanish Bayonet kind which, in bright sun, develops leaves that are broad at the base, stiff, and spine tipped. Having been kept in reflected light, it is now 6 feet high. The stem, except for the leaf scales, looks like that of a dracaena. The leaves have become long and narrow, just like our beaucarnea. So that's a rather strange example of what deprivation different from that of a desert—namely, indoor shade—can do to change the appearance of a plant.

Besides its strange and amusing appearance, the pony tail plant is valuable because it is virtually indestructible. We have heard of dracaenas misbehaving but it would take a cataclysm to harm a beaucarnea in the house. Only three things are necessary—some reflected sunlight, water, and, every few years, a larger pot. Our plant has been in the same container for the last six or eight years, and we would not be surprised if it blew out the sides any day now. We do fertilize occasionally but doubt that it is at all necessary. You can leave it for a couple of months without a drop of water and it will look just as healthy at the end. It will tolerate near-freezing temperatures or your hottest summer day. Of course, it is the larger specimens with thick storage trunks that are most resistant. Young plants should not be that neglected. Shower the leaves and give them a haircut occasionally as the tips have a tendency to turn brown. Decide now to whom to will your pony tail plant.

Once it gets out of the juvenile stage, when it looks like a green spider plant with bulb, Beaucarnea recurvata *begins to look like something else altogether. Here it is with its hair hanging down. Don't try to shear it or you will lose its crowning glory. Indestructible, odd, and beautiful.*

Extraordinary Begonia prismatocarpa, *a golden miniature only ½ inch across.*

11 An Everblooming Miniature Begonia

BEGONIA PRISMATOCARPA

Orchid lovers turn cattleya purple if you suggest that they're anything but ornamental when out of bloom. And if you want to rile a begonia fancier tell him that not *every* one is a beauty. As a matter of fact begonias are an odd group of plants. The ones which are very floriferous are not particularly attractive in leaf or habit. While those that have beautiful leaves present us with watery-looking flowers. Although the many species seem to mimic every kind of leaf, the number that are weedy and uncontrollable is legion. However, since we are not specialists, we can afford to be choosy, and the best of them are stunning. It's just a little difficult, unless you know a lot of them, to find the right ones. That is one of the reasons for the sudden popularity of *Begonia prismatocarpa.* It is new and unmistakably different.

Another reason why this plant has become famous overnight is a change in standards. On the west coast, which has an ideal climate for begonias, they grow like weeds and it is no trick to produce tremendous plants. But 80 percent of our population lives in urban areas in other parts of the country, and what are they to do with these sprawling and hanging giants? So the interest has recently shifted to smaller sizes and even, in the case of *B. prismatocarpa,* gone to the other extreme.

Accustomed to the balmy air of Socotra, an island in the Indian Ocean, prismatocarpa is strictly a terrarium plant when moved to our climate. But, since it is miniature, and terrariums are "in," this is no problem. The plant never grows more than 2 inches high, has leaves which are dark green and crinkled, with an angel-wing shape, and it's a creeper. The flowers have only two oval petals with a spread of almost an inch. They're deep yellow in color—very unusual in begonias—and one of the petals has radiating red lines reaching from the base to the middle.

The demand for prismatocarpa has been so great that small rooted cuttings have been the only plants available—and prices have been the highest per square inch that we can remember for a begonia. No matter. If you give it the right environment you will have no problems. Just fill an old-fashioned glass or snifter half-full of sphagnum moss, press the rooting end of your cutting into it, moisten lightly and cover with clear plastic or glass. Place it in reflected sunlight or at the end of a fluorescent tube. It will start blooming and crawling immediately. The crawl is really something to watch. The tip lifts itself up, throws out aerial roots that drop to the moss and penetrate it and then pull the leaves down. In this way it will soon fill your glass or terrarium and will be so covered with bloom that the leaves will be hardly visible. No other miniature begonia behaves quite like this.

This is a warm grower and, in addition to the humidity, requires temperatures over 65° F. Very little fertilizer is needed. We let it grow for months without any. If the moss needs a watering at all, make up a very mild solution of high phosphorus African violet formula. Cuttings can be taken at any time and will root with ease under cover in moss.

Biophytum sensitivum. *For anyone who needs or delights in miniatures this is a must plant.*

12 False Palm
BIOPHYTUM SENSITIVUM

If we didn't have to worry about the size of house plants our selection of unusual ones would be very different. For instance, there's the baobab tree. Unfortunately it is impossible to have a proper baobab in the house. It's the other way round. How big a house can we put in a baobab tree?

Some people have room for a dwarf palm; others have only space for a midget. As there are no midget palms, you'll have to do with *Biophytum sensitivum*. Some people take this cutey for a mimosa, others for a palm or cycad. It *must* be of the pea family or a cassia. Nope, it's none of these but a very special oxalis.

When the long leaves with their many opposite leaflets are spread out and it is big enough to sport a 1- or 2-inch stem, it is the prettiest little palm tree you've even seen. And out of its center there appears a continuous series of pink five-petaled flowers. After any one of these has lost its petals for a few days, you wake up one morning to find a star-shaped open seedpod lined with dark brown seeds. Wait another hour and they're all gone—slung a distance of up to a yard all over your garden. There they germinate and provide new plants which you can easily dig out of the various pots. It's not at all weedy, but you will always have a supply of plants coming on.

Like all oxalises, biophytum's leaves fold at night. The leaflets assume the position of prayer, and the whole leaf stands more or less straight up or straight down, giving it a decidedly ambiguous sleeping position. But in the morning, bright and early, it gathers its wits and leaves together and makes as pretty a show as you could wish.

Discussing the culture of this oddity is almost a waste of time. All you have to do is keep it reasonably moist and give it some light. Even a north exposure will do or your most unfavorable position under the lights. Fertilizer is unnecessary, and it is indifferent to humidity. Don't dry out for long or let the temperature go below 50°. If you once start growing this charmer, you will soon be giving plants to all your friends.

Bowiea volubilis. *Hardly* volubilis, *this sea onion is sulking.*

13 The Hideous Sea Onion
BOWIEA VOLUBILIS

We usually like a plant because we think it beautiful or curious. We just ignore the ones we consider ugly unless we have learned the lesson that ugliness too has charms. The sea onion is so outstandingly unattractive that, for many people, it becomes "curious." To own it attracts comments like "Why on earth do you want to grow a thing like that?" or "Where did you ever find such a hideous object?" To top it all, it is neither from the sea nor an onion, like the Empire which was neither Holy nor Roman. The dry parts of South Africa are its native soil.

Bowiea volubilis is its name. *Volubilis* in botanical Latin doesn't mean what you think, but twining, an action that it performs when it performs at all. An old name, *Schizobasopsis,* is not a disease but a word compounded of cleft, base, and eye, which gets us exactly nowhere. The sea onion belongs to the lily family, like some of the more respectable succulents.

The sea onion, then, looks just like a very fat, round, smooth, green onion without the pointed tip, which is the remains of leaves—since Bowiea doesn't have those kinds of leaves. The bulb, for such it is, though an aboveground one, may grow five or six inches in diameter. When it's been around awhile, it develops one or more offsets so that the group eventually looks like three or more shiny bald heads in conference. A papery onion skin, which sometimes appears, is removed by most growers in order to exhibit its repellent sheen to best advantage.

In the fall the bulb sends up one or more scraggly, weak, dark green, smooth stems with a good deal of tangled fine asparaguslike foliage. If you do not tie them to a stake they will just flop over the side of the pot. Then, provided good sun or artificial light is available, little greenish white six-petaled flowers, hardly noticeable in the confusion, brighten the stems here and there. It comes as a bit of surprise that it can bloom at all. In summer the stem usually dies down or, rather, collapses.

If this description doesn't send you into ecstasies over our plant, we will be much surprised. Succulent enthusiasts consider it irresistible and

41

almost always have one around—at least as a conversation piece. And that it is. No matter how you try to hide its shame among your plants, your friends will home in on it immediately.

A real merit of *Bowiea volubilis* is that, probably from justifiable embarrassment over its appearance, it is most undemanding and thrives on neglect. Buy a small bulb of the sea onion from a cactus and succulent nursery, plant in Lean Mix, and place it in or near any window or under artificial light. It should receive some indirect sunlight. To the side of the window in a nonpreferred position (more "beautiful" plants deserve the places of honor) or toward the end of a fluorescent tube is good enough for it.

During most of the year treat it very much like a cactus. Water only every couple of weeks and then rather sparingly. If the bulb starts to shrivel, it is a sign that it needs more water. But never soak it, or it will rot. When it starts to grow a stem in early spring, water it thoroughly but allow it to dry out completely between. If you are careful in this regard you may find that your stems and leaves stay green most of the year, especially under lights. Fertilize with a very weak solution of fish emulsion every three months, no more. Don't try for fast growth.

If baby sea onions appear, separate them from the parent and embed them slightly in Cactus and Succulent Mix. Water a very little at a time until they have become well rooted. Brighter light during this process is helpful. Some hard-baked clay kitty litter (or bird gravel) mixed in with the soil and layered on top will give the bulb firmer support in the pot. The plant prefers rather cool temperatures, down to 50° F in winter, but tolerates heat. During cool periods, water even less since the moisture evaporates more slowly and the bulb, being dormant, may rot.

The sea onion goes to town. Green stringy stems which need just such a support as this ingenious trellis. Photo courtesy Geo. W. Park Seed Co.

A reunion of four bald sea onions. Photo courtesy of Thomas H. Everett.

The gay leaves of Calathea makoyana *dance in the sun. At night they fold down at the elbows.*

14 The Peacock Plant
CALATHEA MAKOYANA

A friend of ours was given a magnificent specimen of *Calathea makoyana*, the peacock plant, which had been used as a model for an illustration in a major magazine. She brought it home and gave it tender loving care. But, after a few weeks, it pined and showed signs of debility. Much soul-searching resulted in the conclusion that there must be something wrong with the roots. The leaves were suffering; they came from the roots; ergo, the roots were the source of the evil. The plant was decanted. Horrors. Attached to a number of the roots were fleshy objects, a most sickening white in color, about the size of hazelnuts but oval in shape. All the soil was promptly removed and the offensive growths snipped off. The plant was then repotted with the firm conviction that tumors had been removed and a lingering death avoided. Alas for good intentions. The Calathea expired immediately. What had been removed were normal storage organs of the plant—like a bulb or potato tuber.

Plants grown for foliage in the house and known collectively as marantas include the genera *Calathea, Ctenanthe,* and *Maranta.* The prayer plant, which is a maranta, is the most popular because of its small size and relatively easy culture. Its prayerfulness is nothing unusual as all the marantas change the position of leaves at night, to say nothing of the numerous members of the pea family (cassias, acacias, mimosa, and so on), which do a lot more praying.

43

Among the marantas there are many other real beauties but none, in our opinion, to compare with *Calathea makoyana* from Brazil. The special features of these plants which have attracted the interest of house plant growers are the definite designs that mark the smooth green leaves in contrasting colors, as if they had been painted by an artist. Some have pairs of lines, others regular darker splotches, and a few look as if the design of a whole plant had been drawn on the surface.

Calathea makoyana combines several design themes in a way that is unique for foliage as the coryanthes (see p. 57) is among flowers. The large leaves—they reach 6 inches with good culture—are basically light green above and deep burgundy underneath. On the face of the leaf the designer has laid down a network of fine parallel green lines over a chartreuse surface and pasted on top of that a collage consisting of a stem with short branches and oval leaves in dark green with a touch of burgundy. This form is so sharp and compact that it can be cut out with scissors and suggests a small plant graphically represented.

All around the edge of the leaf is a line that acts as a frame. And, extending at regular intervals from the central stem of the inner design, are curved heavier lines reaching upward. It is interesting to observe that the leaves within the leaves are not all uniform, some being single and some having smaller satellite leaves attached to them. But the whole is a marvel of controlled asymmetry. It is endlessly fascinating to observe the changes in the leaf pattern and the play of light and dark on this leaf.

At least as houseplants all marantas are essentially stemless, the leaves with their long petioles emerging directly from the soil. In some species, however, mature plants do develop flat, jointed, fleshy stems bearing several leaves and capable of rooting at the nodes if pinned down. These never develop, however, into woody trunks.

The calatheas like warm temperatures—over 65° F, constant moisture when in active growth, and high humidity—if possible over 50 percent. Humidifying equipment is usually needed in the house for long-term survival. These are not strictly shade-loving plants as are so many of our foliage houseplants. They will burn if placed in too strong direct sunlight, but they must have strong reflected light or fluorescent light maintained rather close to the tips of the leaves. The medium should be Rich Mix over an inch or more of drainage material—gravel or marble chips—in the bottom of the pot.

A serious cause of loss with these plants is failure to recognize a period of semidormancy. The tubers in the soil are there for a purpose and indicate a season when the weather in their native land is dry for a period. Maranta has a way of reaching a sort of maximum leaf development and then taking a rest. When this happens the pot should be allowed to dry out between waterings and care should be taken to just moisten the soil. Fertilize with high-nitrate solution about once a month.

Marantas can die down to soil level without being actually dead. Moisten once a week and they will, in time, start to sprout again. Cuttings of pseudostems with leaves root rather easily in moist vermiculite in a propagation box. The plant can also be divided.

Just one of the fabulous catasetums, C. fimbriatum. There are a dozen or more flowers on a scape. Many orchids are the most original and variable of all plants.

15 A Vegetable Marksman
CATASETUM FIMBRIATUM

The one chance aspect of pollination mentioned in our digression on pages 102–3 is matched by the one-shot mechanism of *Catasetum*. As a marksman, Billy the Kid would have been no competition for this one. When Darwin described it to Huxley, the latter answered, "Do you really think I can believe all that?" It's easier to believe the absurdity that orchids can think than that they take their sex so seriously.

This weirdy has the stamens protected by a covering or cap from which two antennae hang down, one on each side, to the surface of the lip. One of these is sensitive. When a bee lands on the lip and gives the right kind of nudge to the antenna the cap flies off and the stamens are thrown violently against its body. We've triggered it with a toothpick and seen them fly for a yard through the air. The sticky pad glues itself to the body of the bee in just the right position for pollination of a female flower.

The catasetums certainly are a mixed-up bunch. Some species have double-sexed flowers; in others the male and female organs are on different flowers that don't look at all alike. And there are even plants that produce both single- and mixed-sexed blooms. Botanists really took a tumble on that one, even though they are supposed to know a lot more about the sex of flowers than most of us know of our own. When they found their first catasetums they assumed that the male plants and the female plants were different species. There were a lot of red faces when they discovered the truth at last. In *Catasetum* the male flowers are the attractive ones. Don't worry, though, about trying to get a male flowering plant since the female flowers are produced only under special conditions—rare in cultivation.

Not all catasetums have the spring mechanism. Some are lazy and let the insect do the work. How, within the same genus, there can be such a startling difference is inexplicable. Also there are some flowers that have the lip at the top and others with the lip hanging down. The normal position is lip down, due to the position of the flower on the stem or a twist of 180° that takes place while it is opening. But sometimes these crazy plants (the orchids) will continue on through with a 360° twist so that the lip ends up where it started in the first place. If you examine the ovary, just below the flower, you can see the twist.

The flowers of catasetums range from the grotesque to the supremely beautiful. We grew one type, *Catasetum saccatum*—not a difficult houseplant, by the way—which we illustrate because you just wouldn't believe our description. The lip with its two nostrils is obscenely white with pink spots and drips with fringes—like some sort of flower of evil dreamed up by an artist. It's revoltingly beautiful. *C. fimbriatum* is less formidable and won't give children nightmares. It's a lovely green or yellow spotted with brown and about 2½ inches across. Both these plants produce hanging spikes bearing five to fifteen flowers. *C. pileatum*, which has white and yellow forms, displays a large shiny smooth lip. The whole flower is 3 to 4 inches across and very, very aristocratic. If we didn't know that they are all related by a unique structure, we would think each one belonged to a different family of plants.

Pot the leafless pseudobulbs, with plenty of crock (drainage) in the bottom of the pot, in fir bark mix from an orchid nursery. Keep a little moist and leads will start from the bottom of the bulb, usually one on each side. The leaves grow fast and up to 15 inches long. They are light green, parallel veined, and better-looking than most orchid foliage.

A bee's-eye view of Catasetum saccatum. *Brrrr. Note the hideous maw and the long tusk of the trigger. The leopard skin is fringed. The attraction must be similar to that of the "beauty" to the "beast." The wingspread of this extraordinary flower is 4 inches. That's the anther cap at the top. It flies off when the trigger is disturbed, and the anthers are flung violently against the body of the bee. There they adhere for future pollination of a female flower.*

During growth keep the medium moist and fertilize twice a month with 30-10-10 solution. Keep the plant in reflected bright light or with the leaves just below the fluorescent tubes. The temperature should be above 60° F, for this is one of the warm growing orchids. Growth goes on from late spring until late fall. The leaves reach their maximum length and the pseudobulbs gradually get fat.

The leaves and pseudobulbs, once they've reached maturity, just carry on for a couple of months. Then, depending on the species, from December to February sometime, the flowering stalk appears, lengthens, and eventually blooms. As the stalk gets longer you can raise the plant nearer the lamps since the leaves are no longer important and are on the way out. The flowers go, the leaves drop, and the bulbs become dormant for varying periods. During this time just mist lightly every day or two. Eventually the new lead will show itself.

Catasetum likes high humidity—over 50 percent—but can be misted regularly. However, don't spray as the leaves are very sensitive. The finest mist is what you want. During dormancy, bulbs can be separated and potted up individually. Even a very small back bulb will produce new growths when the time is right.

Once you have grown one *catasetum* you will want to have others. They are great conversation stoppers and a toothpick demonstration of its artillery will stun your guests. Look in catalogs for others of the many exquisite species, most of which make excellent houseplants.

The rosary vine on trellis and in bloom.

16 The Parachute Flowers

CEROPEGIA WOODII AND SANDERSONII

When it comes to odd and varied flowers, the milkweed family runs a close second to the orchids. We know it is very difficult to recognize members of some families until their flowers appear, so surprising are the differences in leaves and growth habit. The milkweed family, on the other hand, includes plants with flowers that appear to have no resemblance to others until we get busy with a magnifying glass. Those of the ceropegias, for instance, mostly from Africa and southeast Asia, don't remind us at all of our common milkweeds. But once there is a seedpod you have the unmistakable proof of the relationship—and this is true of the whole family. That pod, whether long and fat or long and quill-shaped, is stuffed with those same seeds we know so well for their plume of white hairs, and which, as children, we delight in blowing about in the fall. All the ceropegias are strange and make a fine specialized collection not at all difficult to grow.

Ceropegia woodii is the familiar rosary vine, which has long been a houseplant favorite. The stems are as flexible as cotton string and hang straight down from a pot. Its leaves are heart-shaped, about ½ inch in diameter, quite thick, and prettily mottled with green and silver. In a healthily growing plant, round greyish bulblets appear at most of the leaf nodes—hence its common name. If any one of these is removed, you can start a new plant. Such ease of propagation is the nurseryman's delight and one reason why they appear so often in the shops. Notice, by the way, an odd feature of the bulblets. The stem often goes in single at one end and comes out double at the other. Page Charles Addams.

Friends often ask us whether the rosary vine flowers. This should not surprise anyone. There are so many plants around that are grown in the house solely for their foliage that even their owners have the impression they don't bloom at all. This is nonsense of course, for all the higher plants have flowers. It's just a matter of having the right conditions to produce them. In the case of *Ceropegia woodii* the flowers, though not absolutely tiny, are so inconspicuous that people looking directly at the plant miss them. We'll bet that a majority of those who grow it have never seen the flower, sometimes having missed it when blooming.

Flowers they have, and very unusual ones too. They are small, dull, purple inflated bulbs with a rather long syringe or pipe attached and a purple hairy cage set above it. The top looks like the screening on one of those new apartment house chimneys which is meant to catch particles from the incinerator. The whole thing is ¾ inch long and gets lost in the color of the foliage. But, at times, when the plant has lots of them, they make a most interesting and amusing effect.

Look at the flower through a magnifying glass and you'll enjoy it more. As with all or most of the stranger aberrations from normal flowers (those we are used to), this one is a system for insuring cross-pollination. A small insect, forcing its way between the hairs of the cage, suddenly finds itself without support and falls down the slippery sides of the tube onto the sexy parts of the flower. Books tell us this—not how it gets out again. We suspect that, if the prisoner is slow and careful, it can tip the flower tube over on its side and make its egress in comfort. Somehow it has to get out, otherwise it can't continue to another flower and pollinate it.

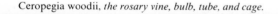

Ceropegia woodii, *the rosary vine, bulb, tube, and cage.*

The giant Ceropegia sandersonii. *One of the most extraordinary of all flower forms.*

Cram Lean Mix into a 2½- or 3-inch pot and plant *C. woodii* with the top of its bulbs even with the surface of the soil. Hang it in a moderately sunny window—an east window will do—and fertilize once a month with fish emulsion. Water whenever the soil becomes dry. For, though it can tolerate drought once its bulblets have grown, it will be larger leaved and more likely to flower if it is kept moist. Maintain 60° or higher temperature. Flowers will appear in spring in the window or at any time under lights. In the light garden, poke a small fan trellis into the pot and wind the stems in and out of the spokes. If the trellis faces toward the tubes, leaves will all face inward and you will soon have a very pretty specimen plant.

Odd and strange as is *C. woodii*, *C. sandersonii* is that to the tenth power. It is a bigger and quite different vine which we grow not for its leaves or bulblets but for its flowers alone. If you get one of these flowers blooming you will cherish the plant forever, for it is really something to show off. Even your condescending relatives will admit you have something special there.

This flower is so complex and three-dimensional that a description in words is unbelievable and perhaps incomprehensible. We'll have a go at it just the same. They are 4 inches high. Starting with a small inflated bulb attached to the pedicel, it expands upward and outward until, at the top, it's over 2 inches across. The five segments of the funnel develop points which support a roof, like a tent, whose five parts are arched upward and which, each segment of the funnel being curved downward at that point, creates five identical large oval-horizontal openings. The points of the roof are decorated with bunches of hairs. The color over all is green and yellow in a design halfway between leopard spotting and the flow of color on a Tiffany vase. The roof is mottled in lighter tones, while the underside is darker. So you really look right through into a room at the level of the windows, though, as far as an insect is concerned, dungeon might be a better word. The whole is usually described as a parachute shape. And that is not too wide of the mark, if one imagines plastic or tissue spread between the strings of the parachute to form a funnel. Whew.

This is a big, unbranching, rapid-growing vine, with green stems and simple, fleshy leaves. Several stems usually grow from the base. The only thing to do with it in the home is to pot it rather large—a 6-incher at least—and train it by force onto a trellis with a diameter of a couple of feet. Use a Lean Mix with lime, keep in half sun, and water regularly. Fertilize once a month with fish emulsion. Both ceropegias do well in the low humidity of an apartment. Cuttings of the stem root easily in moist vermiculite.

It is not always easy to get the ceropegias to grow out well. Sometimes they'll sulk for months, during which time it is wise to cut down on moisture. Then, suddenly, they take off, and you'll have your hands full controlling them. We remember visiting a friend at a time when we were suffering from ceropegia frustration (yes, contrary to most growers, we do have plants that don't always behave) and seeing a pot of the rosary vine sitting on top of a grandfather clock on a landing of his home, where it was lighted by no more than a stained-glass window. The plant almost hid the face of the clock, the leaves were oversize and there were flowers all over the place. It's amazing how so modest a plant, when well grown, can become a spectacular specimen. And we're equally astonished at the frequency with which nonexperts produce plants which make growers with a reputation drool with envy. In indoor gardening everyone has a chance.

The desert grapevine (Cissus quadrangularis) *will keep on crawling, producing a leaf or two at the tips and then losing them. A crazy plant.*

17 The Succulent Grapevine
CISSUS QUADRANGULARIS

There are lots of different kinds of grapevines but none so far which have made the grade growing indoors. However, this does remind us of the manufacturer of an "indoor environment" who must have been pretty desperate to find a sales pitch. In his literature he claimed that you could grow your own wine grapes in his fluorescent-lighted cabinet. You can imagine how intrigued we were. We wrote him asking him for details of culture, etc., since we had visions of starting our own home-grown wine cellar. We suppose there was something wrong because we never had an answer. Perhaps the letter was misdirected. That's part of the fun of knowing your grapevines.

Without benefit of fruit, the family, the *Vitaceae*, has a number of decorative vines for the house. Everybody knows the kangaroo vine, *Cissus antarctica,* or should. It grows like a weed in a hanging basket—in restaurants, hotel lobbies, beauty salons—everywhere. A possibly interesting sidelight is that the public, impressed by size, pays much more for this and similar plants that grow quickly for the nurseryman, than it does for much more beautiful ones of smaller dimensions that have taken a long time to reach maturity. The prices paid for them sometimes have us gasping.

Truly beautiful is *Cissus discolor* which, unfortunately, has never been well housebroken. The teardrop leaves have wonderful veinings and markings which are silvery, purplish, and iridescent with touches of brilliant red. Requiring high humidity, warmth, and miles to run in, it's a toughy, though not impossible for someone who has a sunny window and is willing to spray the plant a couple of times a day plus training it to manageable proportions. Possibly it's the most gorgeous of the foliage vines. If you see it, you won't resist the temptation to try.

But our concern here is not conventional beauty but oddity and here comes the unbelievable one of the family—the nonconformist *Cissus quadrangularis*—a succulent from tropical Africa and Asia. With its bizarre appearance, we had a little trouble identifying an unlabeled specimen the first time we saw it. Consulting the botanical literature we made a couple of false starts and then homed in on the foliage which consisted of a single small leaf at each node. That gave us the clue, for they were pure grape. Imagine a stem, square in cross section, sometimes ½ an inch in diameter, with nodes about 1 inch apart, standing straight up—and with these incongruous grape leaves sticking out at intervals. It's a wild, fun plant.

Out in its desert home it grows several feet long and high by supporting itself on larger shrubs and succulents. We've seen short tendrils on it, like those of a normal grapevine, and it might succeed by leaning. Being rather stiff it can keep going straight up until it finds a branch to lean on. Having secured sufficient purchase it may reach up for the next branch. We suppose, though we've never tried it, that it could be trained to grow onto a dried branch of a shrub stuck into a pot, and that it would look rather interesting that way. A trellis would be a good support but unsuitable aesthetically. Some people and plants look best when you conform to their habits. Quadrangularis is an untidy plant and should have the proper untidy surroundings.

In the house we usually don't want to let this curious plant just grow and grow. So, when a single stem has reached a desirable height, we trim it back, seeking to stimulate growth lower down the stem. Alas, this kills all the leaves for good. However, the next lower node produces a branch with leaves—a branch that grows straight up just like the lower part. Meanwhile the cut-off piece is rooted in any moist medium like Lean Mix and soon takes off on its own. One thing we can say for it, it's one fast-growing succulent. Incidentally, when taking a cutting, be careful not to turn it upside down in planting. It won't grow downward, but it won't grow upward either.

You can use any kind of garden soil (sterilized) or Lean Mix. Quadrangularis will thrive in good indirect sunlight and, if kept moist, will develop big, fat segments. Growth is very rapid—about a segment every two weeks and the leaf appears right away at the node. Actually the node can produce two leaves, one on each side, but one of these is aborted. Temperatures can go down to the forties and humidity is unimportant. Extreme heat does not bother it. *Cissus quadrangularis* takes up a minimum of room and always elicits astonishment from those who have never seen it before.

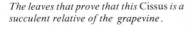

The leaves that prove that this Cissus *is a succulent relative of the grapevine.*

The coffee plant makes a handsome small indoor tree. The leaves are unusually dark green and shiny.

Grow Your Own Coffee
COFFEA ARABICA

If you work at it you can not only grow a little coffee tree in the house but collect a harvest of beans. Unless you have room for several big tubs of this handsome little tree, there won't be that many beans, but you can still experiment with any you do have by drying them, roasting them, and then brewing your own—enough for four thimblefuls in all probability. Not very productive, but still a sporting challenge. If successful you can throw a coffee party for the occasion, with extra brew on hand for those whose thirst is not satisfied by a few drops of novelty.

All you require is one of the commercially grown *Coffea arabica* plants which are readily available at nurseries and garden centers. Plenty of people buy them but seem to have the idea that a tree in the house needs no attention, least of all water—accounting for no beans. A few hours of sunlight each day and a house which is never colder than 60° in winter are the other requirements. Most of the plants are only 6-to-8-inchers in 4-inch pots. They will bloom in late summer even at that size, with pleasant white, five-petaled, fragrant flowers in clusters.

Don't expect to produce beans early in the life of the tree. According to the growers three years to fruiting is the minimum. Grow them on and move to larger pots, trimming every so often to make them bushy. Use Rich Mix and be careful not to let the plants stand in water. They don't have to dry out between waterings but must not be soggy, especially in cooler weather or when there is a spell of cloudiness. Fertilize during the spring and summer months with high-nitrate fertilizer at one quarter the strength recommended. In winter fertilize every couple of weeks.

54

A coffee shrub in flower. The little white flowers are fragrant.

Here's the real coffee bean enjoying itself before drying and roasting begins. These beans will end up on somebody's breakfast table and wake him up some morning.

If leaves develop brown edges with this treatment, switch to high-potash fertilizer and move to a less well lighted position. On commercial plantations taller trees are planted among the coffee trees in order to shade them. Which reminds us: People often seem to feel that they are uniquely unfortunate when a plant of this sort fails in the house. It must be their own brown thumbs or the unsuitability of the plant. They should remember that in nature or when grown with the greatest care on plantations, such trees sometimes fail to set fruit and sometimes suffer serious damage from the weather. The price of coffee is partly a reflection of good and bad crops in Brazil, where nature is not always bountiful any more than in the home.

When your tree can be moved to an 8-to-12-inch pot and is 18 or more inches high, you can try to get some beans. Take a few-haired camel's hair brush and pick up pollen from some of the flowers and dust all around on the others. Do this also as more flowers open up, just like any good working bee. In the fall the plant should then develop ½-inch pink or red fruit, which turns black after a while and shrivels. Some varieties of coffee flower and fruit off and on throughout the year. When the fruit dries up, harvest it and remove the two seeds inside. Those are coffee beans. Dry thoroughly in the air, roast in a pan until they smell like coffee, grind in your mill (coffee, but for small quantities a pepper grinder will do), and brew.

A hanging cluster of Coryanthes speciosa var. maculata. *Luna Park for a species of bee. The flower at three o'clock clearly shows the spigot and the cap and bucket. Petals and sepals, which don't contribute to the mechanism, are just furled away.* Photo courtesy of Richard Peterson and the American Orchid Society.

19 The Oddest Flower in the World

CORYANTHES SP.

Of this orchid, a major nursery in its catalog remarks, "Remarkably complex floral structure, indescribable in lay terms." We are glad we can include a photograph, although even looking at that won't clear up all the mysteries. As you can see, this one has none of the characteristics we are accustomed to associate with the word *flower.*

It is one of the helmet orchids, genus *Coryanthes,* that inhabit rain forests in Venezuela, Guiana, and Brazil. Of all the mechanisms for trapping insects for the purpose of cross-fertilization, these are probably the most complex. In fact the whole flower has been distorted in the service of a particular course of events that happens to the visiting bee and forces it to contribute its bit to the continuation of the species.

Observe the club-shaped affair on the end of a stalk. The bee is attracted to it by a highly intriguing odor. The bee lands and tears at the surface with its powerful foreclaws releasing a sap, which it imbibes. The effect has been estimated as equivalent to three jiggers of VSO Brandy before eating. Bee falls into bucket in a state of intoxication. Bucket contains controlled amount of water which has been dripping from tap above. The liquid is sufficient to sober bee but not to drown it. Bee comes to and searches for means of egress. It sees a ray of light and pushes its way forcefully through a perfectly constructed pressure valve.

The incredible Coryanthes. This is C. bungerothii *Behind the cap there seems to be a ladder to assist the bee in reaching the cap. Next it falls into the bucket.* Photo courtesy of Thomas H. Everett.

Coryanthes rodriguezzi *attracting a bee. In this photo the escape valve is clearly shown on the right side of the bucket. As a matter of fact its somewhat shaggy look may have been due to the exiting of this bee, which is probably recovering from the experience.* Photo courtesy of Richard Peterson and the American Orchid Society.

In the process it picks up the masses of pollen as it shoots out into space. In spite of is traumatic experience, it succumbs to the attraction of another flower. It repeats the process. This time, in passing through the valve it leaves its load of pollen on the stigmatic surface and picks up a new load. So it goes, on and on, until the bee is exhausted and curls up on a leaf to sleep.

Each species of coryanthes is adapted to a particular local bee. If it is too big it will escape the bucket, and if too small will go through the orifice without picking up or depositing the pollen. There are all kinds of shapes and colors to the flowers, from polka dots on pink to combinations of brown, yellow, orange, and red. The flowers are about 3 inches across and hang in pairs on pendent wishbone-shaped stems. The pseudobulbs are pear-shaped and have two leaves growing out of the top.

Well, we're cheating with this one. Everywhere else in this book we have been careful to describe plants that are not too difficult for you to grow in the house. Coryanthes is such an altogether crazy one that we include it for sheer entertainment. Of course it is just possible to grow it in the home. All it needs is a basket full of epiphytic orchid mix, a humidity level approximating that of a Turkish bath, temperatures of 65° or better, and fertilization with high-phosphate solutions. Oh, yes. It needs full sunlight too. If you have all that you can grow coryanthes. We wouldn't even try.

Zamia floridana, *one of our handsome native "fossil" plants. It's gone through so much in millions of years of change that it will put up with a remarkable amount of mistreatment. A splendid foliage plant for a sunny corner.*

20 Living Fossils
THE CYCADS

Of recent years we have become accustomed to the idea of living fossils since the sensational rediscovery of the coelacanth, the planting of large numbers of gingko trees in our city streets, and the cultivation of cycads in pots. Actually these "fossils" are by no means uncommon in the plant world. Many of the lower plants have changed little in millions of years. When whole races of animals and plants were massacred by changes in world weather, a certain number always managed to escape and carry on. That is why there are still cycads around; they are the most primitive of seed plants.

Cycads look superficially like a primitive palm, and you will undergo a shock of recognition if you are familiar with reconstructions of forests of the carboniferous age. Some are tall and have naked stems but most are relatively low with long arching fronds. Where they differ most obviously from palms is in the leaflets of the fronds, which lack a midvein, and in the fruit, which always arises in the center of the fountain of fronds and may look like a single large pineapple. Some of these fruits are very striking in texture and color and may weigh twenty or more pounds.

Recently young cycads in pots have become popular because they are decorative, very slow-growing, and can take a great deal of neglect without succumbing completely. One of the smaller species is *Zamia*

LIBRARY

JOHN D. PIERCE

REDFORD, MICHIGAN 48239

floridana which can easily be kept in a 10-inch pot for a long time and has relatively few leaflets per frond. Then there is *Dioon edule* with ostrichlike plumes and *Cycas circinalis* and *revoluta* just about in between. The last three and *Encephalartos*, an African plant, can develop an enormous spread but take so long to do that in the house that you won't have to worry about it.

These plants can be placed in either partial or full sunlight and will exist, though not flourish, quite far back from a window or under ceiling fluorescent lights in an office. They need watering only when thoroughly dry and, if you have neglected them entirely, will come back to life and put out new fronds even if the old ones die off from thirst. Give them high-nitrate fertilizer every three months. If you want them to be more lush and grow a little faster, keep them warm, spray the leaves often, and keep the soil moist. The plants do all right in ordinary garden soil, but well-packed Lean Mix is to be preferred.

As juveniles, cycads of the genus Cycas *make handsome ferny-palmy foliage plants.*

Young plant of Dioon edule, *one of the most beautiful of the cycads.*

Encephalartos, *another cycad, is a very spiny plant. But look at that mar-velous mealy-musty center.*

This will give you an idea of an adult Dioon edule *in fruit. That center is well over a foot across and magnificently fuzzy.*

Miniature papyrus in a pot. Cyperus alternifolius nanus.

21 Your Own Indoor Papyrus
CYPERUS ALTERNIFOLIUS NANUS

Grow your own papyrus. Make your own *Book of the Dead*—or almost. Our small papyrus plant is not quite that productive, but you might be able to make a miniature page by collecting a lot of stems and following instructions from one of the pyramids. *Cyperus alternifolius,* a swamp denizen of Madagascar, is a delightful small relative of the giant grass of the Nile. The latter grows 8 feet high and our plant to 4 feet. But variations available from nurseries are dwarfs that reach a maximum of 1½ feet and so are manageable in the house.

The single stems are topped by an arching spray of very narrow leaves which has earned it the name of umbrella plant. They are often available at garden centers or can be ordered from aquatic plant nurseries.

Plant in a ceramic or glass container in 3 or 4 inches of soilless mix—Lean Mix preferably—with some sand added. Pour in enough water to cover the soil to the depth of an inch and set the pot in the window. Don't use any lime. If you prefer, cyperus can be planted in an ordinary clay pot with a hole and the bottom constantly immersed in water. The soil must never dry out. The water should contain a mild dilution of 20-10-10 or similar high-nitrate fertilizer. About one tenth the recommended strength is right. Maintain the temperature constantly above 55° F. You may have to mist daily to prevent browning of the leaves.

When cyperus has several stems, it can be divided. Another method of propagation is to take a leaf with a short piece of stem and float it on water. Plantlets grow at the base of the segments of leaf which you can pot up separately. This is a great plant around which to build little water gardens in the house.

This drosera is living off the fat of the land, as you can see. Also you get an idea of the smallness of the insects. So don't try to feed yours too heavily. This is Drosera capensis. Photo courtesy of Thomas H. Everett.

22 The Sundew
DROSERA SPECIES

The sundews or droseras are so tropical-looking that we would expect to find them growing only in a rain forest. On the contrary, they are as common everywhere in moist places of the temperate zone and a number of species can tolerate freezing winters. If sheer numbers are significant, they are certainly among the most successful of carnivorous plants. All sundews, whether their leaves are threadlike, spoon-shaped, or round, are armed with sticky hairs that trap insects and digest them.

This trick is a marvel of the plant world, and it is a shame that we don't all have microscopes capable of watching the process take place step by step. The trapping operation is not mechanical—not even muscular as in the Venus-flytrap—but a controlled growth process.

Each hair covering the leaves is tipped with a viscous, gluey liquid that attracts insects as a source of nectar. As soon as they land, the sticky stuff holds them down and the nearby hairs start to curve inward over the victim, holding him fast. The hairs do not just move—they grow. For the cells on the side of each hair opposite to the insect start to grow longer while those on the inner side do not change. This causes the hair to bend. It is as simple as that. Once the insect is enclosed, the liquid exuded by the hairs breaks down its tissues and the plant absorbs and digests the protein content. When digestion is completed, the inner side of the hair begins to grow while the outer now remains unchanged. So the hair straightens up again. The process takes several days.

Obviously there is a limit to the number of times the trick can work. Otherwise the hair would just get longer and longer. Two or three feedings are all a leaf can manage before exhaustion sets in and other leaves must take over the job.

It is difficult to account for a mutation that would adapt a plant to a protein diet. But the reason is suggested by the fact that the sundews live in sphagnum moss and wet sandy soils, which are very poor in nutrients. Plants often invade inhospitable regions to get away from competition. Perhaps the same instinct causes us to seek out deserted islands. In life you either fight or run, and sundews have chosen to run—and adapt. They are by no means dependent on insects for food, but will thrive in soils that will nourish them.

The sundew we usually grow indoors is the round-leaved—*Drosera rotundifolia*—which is small—a 1-inch-high rosette—but has neat five-petaled flowers large in comparison with the rest of the plant. It is odd that, though the round-leaved sundews are about the same size from Maine to Florida, the threadleaf sundew *(Drosera filiformis,* or dew thread) varies greatly. In the North the latter are at most 4 inches high with ⅜-inch flowers, while in the Florida Panhandle they are among the showiest of spring flowers. In the moist swales that divide the roads from the forests that supply pulpwood grow millions of dew threads up to 10 inches high, with gorgeous 1-inch-wide pure pink flowers. In the morning light, with every beaded hair reflecting the sun and every flowering stem with its pink flower, the roadsides are like a cloud suffused with glowing pink.

About noon the show is over. The flower opens in the morning and times itself. Maybe the plant doesn't want the flowers, which have the function of propagating the species, to interfere all day with the activity of the leaves. After pleasure (read sex) comes food. On one occasion we came across a particularly fine colony of round-leaved sundews, which we wanted to photograph. As soon as we had the camera set up and tried to focus, the flower would close. When we moved to another one the same thing happened. We suddenly realized that twelve o'clock had struck, that lunch was due, and that we would never be able to guess which of the many flowers was ready to shut now or give us a few extra minutes of its time. But we did stay long enough to observe them all close within a period of about fifteen minutes.

Contrary to the advertisements of the carnivorous plant nurseries, these plants are not all that easy to grow. They will last for a while, but keeping them for over six or eight months requires some skill. They require very high humidity, a very porous and rather sterile soil, constant moisture, and, though tolerant of cold outdoors, a temperature in the house that is over 60° throughout the year. This means maintaining them in a terrarium. Being such small plants a brandy snifter 6

Business is not as good for this thread-leaf type of sundew, Drosera dichotoma. *Photo courtesy of Thomas H. Everett.*

Flower of a beautiful variety of Drosera filiformis *from the Florida panhandle.*

inches in diameter is sufficient for a small clump. The rosettes are only a couple of inches across. The best medium is sphagnum moss over a bed of pebbles. Next is plain wet bog sand—not seashore sand. Don't try them in potting soil. Very light peaty mixes, such as our Lean Mix, will do in a pinch but are not ideal. Roots are very shallow and you need only to press the plant into the wet sphagnum or sand to anchor it.

Sundews can stand high temperatures but can be suffocated. Setting your terrarium in good reflected light, not direct sunlight, will avoid overheating. On very hot, humid days the top of the terrarium can be opened a bit to let in some fresh air. Don't fertilize. If you can feed, do so. Fruit flies are fair game but it is hard to find other food for them in the house. If the insect is too big the plant will get indigestion. It doesn't work any better than trying to feed chopped meat to Venus-flytraps. A drop of beef juice on a leaf, however, is appreciated. Or reduce your dose of chopped meat to the size of a pinhead, which is not easy. Without this protein nourishment the plant will survive but not attain maximum vigor.

Provided there is good light, sundews bloom, throwing up one stalk after another, and often set seed. With time you may have a number of rosettes growing close together. Any one of these can be moved to a new terrarium home.

The sight of these gleaming, perfectly symmetrical reddish rosettes of sparkling leaves is a thing of considerable beauty—and a conversation piece.

The fantastic foliage of Episcia *'Cleopatra.'*

23 Episcia 'Cleopatra'

If there is one plant which, more than any other, will create a sensation in an indoor garden it is *Episcia* 'Cleopatra.' It is not just odd but gorgeous, and it is gorgeous in a way that is unique. Variegation in foliage is common among cultivated plants. Nurserymen are always looking for it because the public likes it and for good reason. A very ordinary green leaf is transfigured by the addition of spots or stripes of another color. What was just another piece of greenery becomes strikingly decorative. Sometimes the results are not that good, and the combinations of colors are really quite drab. Nevertheless the average plant buyer will always go for a variegated-leaf plant in preference to a plain one. What makes *Episcia* 'Cleopatra' so extraordinary is that the colorings are so clear, so unusual, and so gay, giving the plant the appearance of a mass of spectacular bloom.

According to the story, Easterbrook's Greenhouses in Butler, Ohio, were growing in 1962 an *Episcia* cultivar called 'Frosty,' which had velvety green leaves and a silver midstripe. 'Frosty' was only one of the numerous variations that have turned up in the cultivation of *Episcia cupreata* from Central America. Well, one day, Mr. Easterbrook found a plant among many normal ones which, in the official description, had a "pink leaf with a green mid-section shaped like an oak leaf, surrounded with a thin halo of white. Bright red flowers." The edging of the leaf is soft pink and this color scallops in and out of the white area as irregular spots on the quilted surface.

It is quite obvious that 'Cleopatra' hasn't quite got all its marbles. It isn't an albino, as one might expect, for the flower is brightly colored. But with all that white and pink there is very little green color left for photosynthesis. So maybe anemia is a better diagnosis. Nevertheless the leaves grow to normal size—3 to 5 inches—and are firm and crisp. Cuttings propagate easily in moist vermiculite in a propagation box. The plant does not require terrarium conditions.

If a bit more difficult to grow than some other episcias, 'Cleopatra' is very well within the capability of the average amateur. Still the spectacular coloring appears to be responsible for some of the problems encountered in growing it. Like albinoid people it is more sensitive to light and more delicate than some of its relatives. For instance it needs more light but is more easily scorched than others. We remember an occasion when we photographed a plant using powerful flood lamps. With just two or three minutes of exposure the whole upper layer of leaves turned brown and, though we removed these promptly, it sulked for days thereafter since we didn't have the right brand of suntan lotion with which to treat it.

'Cleopatra' is also more dependent on high humidity but rots out in a closed atmosphere. It wants to be moist but, if the temperature drops below 65°, stem rot can set in. It is an extremely slow grower. Apparently, though, if we avoid extremes and observe a few rules of care it will survive under normal house conditions especially if grown under fluorescent light.

Pot 'Cleopatra' in Rich Mix, packing it firmly but not tightly. Keep in a room that has a minimum of 50 percent humidity and a temperature that rarely if ever falls below 65° F. Maintain constant moisture and feed with high-phosphate–potash formula. It is happiest in good reflected light or at the ends of the fluorescent tubes at a distance of 5 inches. It prefers to be overpotted. Wide azalea pots are best as the root system is shallow. The problem in growing 'Cleopatra' lies principally in the watering. Never allow it to dry out completely and never let it get soggy. This means giving it water in relatively small doses, preferably from the bottom, and letting it soak up what it needs. We have found that it looks best when all stolons are cut off (they can be used to propagate) and all the leaves form a solid mass in the pot.

An episcia flower. This one is of E. *'Moss Agate.'*

The leaves of the lilac episcia, E. lilacina, *combine gorgeous greens with the texture of Turkish toweling.*

The cultivar 'Ember Lace' has some similarity to 'Cleopatra' but is less attractively marked and has a tendency to revert.

Episcia 'Cleopatra' is such a choice and beautiful plant that neglecting it is inconceivable. When you have a spread of a foot or more, the coloring can vie with the finest of your blooming plants.

While we are on the subject we take the opportunity of advising you to become acquainted with the episcias which are handsome members of the African violet, or gesneriad, family. The episcias are valued for exquisite foliage and small but very brightly colored flowers. The leaves are simple ovals, ranging in length from 3 to 6 inches on longish thick petioles. What makes them unmistakable is the variety of patterns and textures in combinations of green and brown. There are heavy veinings and quiltings. There are leaves with a pile so thick that they look like new cotton washcloths. Many have a rich silvery sheen. The flowers, about an inch in length, have flared tubes with simple or fringed lobes, mostly in tints of tomato red but also in pink and yellow and white. There is even a blue-flowered species, *Episcia lilacina,* with oversize flowers, which is very difficult to grow in the house.

Brought into cultivation in gardens of their native countries of Central America, and in American nurseries, the species have interbred naturally and been crossed artificially. In addition, among a large number of plants and under different cultural conditions, new leaf colors and textures appear from time to time—like 'Cleopatra.' The plant is now so civilized that, like African violets, nobody thinks in terms of species anymore; they are almost all cultivars—artificially bred plants. Many of these have become standard and very attractive house-plants.

Weird distortion in a euphorbia, E. lactea, *is a common occurrence. The violent branchings make interesting sculptural pieces with a touch of menace.*

24 A Horrid Euphorbia

EUPHORBIA LACTEA CRISTATA

Cresting is an abnormality that occurs frequently in succulents, some species being more subject to it than others. The cause may be a virus, damage done by insects, or, perhaps, radiation. Don't get it confused with etiolation, an odd word applied to those stringy growths you get on cacti when they don't have enough light. In cresting, the leafy or succulent section of the plant becomes distorted—splits and twists and fans out in a grotesque way. It is of frequent occurrence in the cacti *Opuntia clavarioides, O. cylindrica, Cereus peruvianus, Mammilaria elongata, Echinopsis tubiflora, and Rebutia minuscula.* There is something cancerous about the appearance of these growths and we do not like them at all. On the other hand cactus and succulent enthusiasts often dote on them and collect examples, the more frightful the better. The real whopper and horror of them all is *Euphorbia lactea cristata.*

Euphorbia lactea is a large plant, almost a tree, from the East Indies, with leafless angled branches, vicious short spines, and a white stripe along the center of each surface. In the crested form, all simple branching disappears, and the plant becomes a gnarled, twisted mass of greenery with innumerable spreading points and surfaces. Specimens of this ugly plant come in large tubs and may be 3 to 4 feet high and as much across. They cost a small fortune. A 6-incher to start with will be priced at ten dollars or more.

From a small beginning, if you are blessed with patience and a long life, you can grow a large specimen of this plant in the house without any difficulty. Smaller examples are sufficiently representative to satisfy your desire for something extra hideous. Culture is almost a matter of neglect. They will do in any kind of poor soil or in Lean or Cactus and Succulent Mix. Water very sparingly and fertilize not more than four times a year with fish emulsion. Good sun and near dryness most of the time preserve the crestate form. Give too much water and ordinary growths appear. Cut them off or your oddity will start to grow normally, which will never do. The scars contribute to the tortured appearance of the plant.

This is an excellent piece of living sculpture for an odd corner. It is, in fact, a favorite of institutions where nobody would ever think of watering anything—because it isn't their job. Under such conditions, *cristata* may last for several years with no visible change in appearance except the gradual accumulation of dust on its surface.

A beautiful example of Euphorbia obesa. Photo courtesy of Thomas H. Everett.

25 A Beautiful Fatty
EUPHORBIA OBESA

To the loveliest fat object we can think of in the plant world even the botanist who first described it was compelled to apply the name *Euphorbia obesa.* No other has quite that shape or is graced at the same time with such colors.

What an extraordinary family are the euphorbias! A renowned plant encyclopedist asked us one day to name the most varied of families. We didn't suggest our first thought, the orchids, because the differences there are remarkable only in the flower. So we opted for the milkweed family. "Nope," said our friend, "it's the euphorbias." That was a subjective choice, of course, as any choice must be. But it may be true. Consider all the succulent euphorbias which are like cacti and others like brambles, the gorgeous poinsettia, the crotons, the chenille plant. And what about those lacy mats that grow on seashore dunes or snow-on-the-mountain and its relatives, which are common in our gardens or in our forests. Truly the euphorbia has adjusted itself to innumerable different climatic and soil conditions.

Even among euphorbias, *E. obesa* is unique. Of it Edgar Lamb *(Cacti and Other Succulents,* Vol. 1) writes, "This is perhaps *the* finest Euphorbia yet known." Like most of the interesting euphorbia succulents, it comes from South Africa. Indeed, what would the horticultural world

71

do without South Africa? The lack would precipitate a crisis, since so many of the interesting, weird, and lovely plants come from there.

A fine example of *E. obesa* measures 4 inches across and perhaps 5 to 5½ inches high. That isn't much in terms of dimensions. But the only really great other fatty we can think of is the baobab tree which is a monster, indeed, and not something you would want to tackle.

Our plant doesn't look like a plant at all. It resembles a geodesic dome, so perfect is its symmetry. The pineapple shape—broader at the base and gently curving to a rounded top—is divided longitudinally into ten sections. In cross section it is perfectly decagonal. The surface is smooth and shimmering all over. The ridge of each wedge has a fine regular beading running its length consisting of alternate light and dark spots. The surfaces are patterned like the finest cloth, with delicate lines of the threads angled evenly downward from the ridges. Fainter horizontal lines run from top to bottom. The color is a mixture, to quote again, "of purple, green, red, mauve, etc." The *etc.* covers all kinds of pastel tints. Thus the overall effect is marvelously iridescent, and the whole plant possesses a warm glow.

Small plants can be bought from succulent nurseries for as little as $3. Large examples may cost ten or more times that much and are worth it. The plant will live as long as you, with proper care. The small yellowish green flowers grow in a cluster on the top but add nothing to the appearance.

Give it the best sun you have and water every two weeks in warm weather. Water lightly not more than once a month in winter. To preserve this valuable plant from danger of rotting where the base is in contact with moist soil, we use a trick. We remove about ⅜ of an inch of soil all around the base and replace it with fine gravel mixed with some clay to give it firmness. No regular fertilizer is necessary but a mild treatment with fish emulsion every six months will do it good. Your only risk is overwatering.

The fabulous Euphorbia obesa. *We illustrate this specimen for its "nipples" along the ridge of the sections and its crop of seedpods.* Photo courtesy of P. R. Chapman, A.R.P.S.

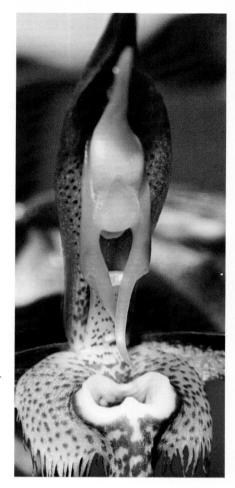

A VEGETABLE MARKSMAN: *Catasetum saccatum*.

THE GIANT CARRION FLOWER: *Stapelia variegata*. Note the odd annular ring.

THE PARACHUTE FLOWER: *Ceropegia sandersonii*. One of the most fantastic of all flowers.

EPISCIA 'CLEOPATRA.'

THE BLUSHING AIR PLANT: *Tillandsia ionantha.*

A LIVING FOSSIL: *Encephalartos horridus.* Huge cycad fruit.

TROPICAL SUNDAE FLOWER: *Aechmea fasciata*.

DARWIN'S ORCHID: *Angraecum sesquipedale*. Photo courtesy Donald Richardson.

THE INCREDIBLE ALOE: *Aloe sp.*

FOXTAIL ASPARAGUS: *Asparagus meyeri*. Photo courtesy Geo. W. Park Seed Co.

AN EVERBLOOMING MINIATURE BEGONIA: *Begonia prismatocarpa*.

THE PONY TAIL PLANT: *Beaucarnea recurvata*.

THE RAINBOW CACTI: *Gymnocalcium sp.*

FLOWER OF THE WAX PLANT: *Hoya bella.*

THE LEAFY CACTUS: *Pereskia aculeata*. The lemon vine.

THE POLKA DOT PLANT: *Hypoestes sanguinolenta.*

THE BLACK LEAF ORCHID: *Ludisia discolor.*

THE GIANT PANSY: *Miltonia Limelight 'Imogene.'* Photo courtesy of Donald Richardson.

THE FEATHERY FERNS: *Nephrolepis 'norwoodii.'* A fine-leaved Boston fern.

THE BEAD PLANT: *Nertera depressa.* Photo courtesy of T. H. Everett.

THE FUR BLANKET: *Polypodium aureum.*

MINIATURE JADE TREE: *Portulacaria afra-variegata.*

PEACOCK SELAGINELLA: *Selaginella uncinata.*

THE SEA ONION: *Bowiea volubilis.* Photo courtesy Geo.
W. Park Seed Co.

The miniature crown of thorns starts blooming early in life.

26 Crown of Thorns

EUPHORBIA SPLENDENS BOJERI

The popular crown of thorns would not be included here save for the oddity of its house manners. One expects a succulent to bloom once a year or, at most, occasionally if you treat it right. But, if you treat crown of thorns right, it will bloom continuously. For this reason it is one of the best of our blooming houseplants. However, it is not enough to buy a plant called crown of thorns or *Euphorbia splendens*. It must be the variety *bojeri* or at least be called the miniature crown of thorns. This is not so difficult a requirement as it seems, for the simple reason that *bojeri* is the kind usually sold in variety stores. There are also heavier-stemmed novelty hybrids with much larger flowers and more of them in a cluster. They are handsome, no doubt, but don't behave nearly as well in the house.

The crown of thorns was named of course because of its thorniness, which is quite horrific. It is a South African bramble that can attain considerable size and form impenetrable barbed-wire areas. The smaller plants, though equally thorny, are easy to handle and of nearly foolproof culture.

As you know, the poinsettia—also a euphorbia—owes its spectacular

Because they keep them dry, you will not see the crown of thorns (Euphorbia bojeri) *in a botanical garden. Here it is as leafy as any nonsucculent. The red flowers make a brilliant contrast.*

appearance to big rosettes of red leaves at the tops of the stems. The true flowers are those little yellow cups bunched in the center. In the same way, though on a much smaller scale, *Euphorbia bojeri* flowers are tiny but are flanked by two half-rounds of deep pink or brick red bracts. Each peduncle produces one to three flowers. In a botanical garden you often see specimens of the big crown of thorns rambling against a wall, bearing canes several feet long, usually nearly leafless and bearing a few flowers. Our little *bojeri*, on the other hand, is a very leafy plant with nice spoon-handle-shaped leaves which quite hide the vicious thorns beneath.

But your plant will stay green and bloom only if you break every rule in the treatment of succulents and virtually drown it. It must be very moist at all times and you need never fear, with a mature plant, to have water in the saucer as long as the temperature is over 65° F. and it has a fair amount of light. Withdraw the water or give it a couple of dry days and the leaves will fall like the maples' in autumn and flowering will stop for a long time.

The light requirement is surprisingly low. In a window you may have to give it nearly full sunlight, largely because of the off and on cloudy days. But under lights it does far better than one would expect from such a desert plant. In fact fluorescent light culture is far more reliable. Just keep it within a few inches of the lights at all times.

Pot *Euphorbia bojeri* in Lean Mix with lime and fertilize it with fish emulsion when watering. Since it grows rather rapidly it is advisable to prune it and make it branch. In this way it is possible to shape it into a handsome candelabrum. Nipping also encourages bloom.

When you cut a piece of branch both ends of the cut will bleed like the devil with a pure white milky sap. Put a flaming match to both bleeding ends in order to cauterize them. The cuttings can be planted in Lean Mix and will root within a short time.

74

They're looking at you. Fenestraria rhophalophylla *stems with "windows" at the top. In the South African desert the eyes are even with the soil.*

27 The Window Plant

FENESTRARIA AURANTIACA AND RHOPALOPHYLLA

In the deserts of South Africa, where the sun is of violent intensity, a number of succulents have developed a device to filter and reduce the amount of sunlight reaching the active chlorophyll layer on which they depend for life and growth. Much of the exposed parts of these plants is light resistant, or they bury themselves in the soil for protection. Part of the exposed surface, however, consists of cells without chlorophyll which are like windows, permitting the sun in reduced quantities to reach the chlorophyll layer deep in the leaves.

There is an interesting mystery here. Many succulents live in arid areas of the Americas and are subjected to similar light intensities yet have not evolved this method of combating the glare. Why should this be? It would be more understandable if the feature were confined to one family. But that is not the case and in South Africa examples are to be found in a number of them. For instance *Haworthia cymbiformis,* an attractive succulent of the lily family, possesses vertical rows of these windows in its fleshy leaves.

So the fenestrarias are not the only species with this oddity. We choose it because it is a more unusual-looking plant and also, perhaps, for the reason that its name means window. They are related to the Living Stones, which we describe on page 97, and live almost totally buried in the hard hot soil with only a little dome of nose showing—or

75

perhaps an eyelike window would be a better simile. A very hard life indeed—for the burning heat of midday is succeeded at nightfall by a drastic drop in temperature, so the poor things freeze the rest of the time. So totally are such plants adapted to survival that, when we have managed to destroy everything else, they may still be goggling at the sky, unnoticed grey green bumps on the soil. We might liken them to science fiction houses buried in the moon soil with only their windows showing.

The two most cultivated fenestrarias, which look much alike, are *F. aurantiaca* with orange flowers and *F. rhopalophylla* with white flowers. These are surprisingly large 2-inchers with many petals. The leaves are club-shaped, about an inch long, and form clusters, all standing straight up, with their pop eyes all staring and obviously transparent. Buried, except for the tip, in their native deserts, we grow them in the home with their leaves exposed, because of the ever-present danger of excess moisture. In this way we can also enjoy their pretty blue grey coloration and odd stumpy form.

Fenestraria dislikes root disturbance. If you start with seeds, plant two or three to a pot on top of the soil which should be our Lean Mix. Allow the pot to soak up moisture from the bottom and cover with a glass or plastic. Remove the glass after the seedlings are well up. Flowering takes place in August-September and growth is from March till the end of flowering. During growth, water once every two weeks. During winter don't water at all. Don't fertilize. House temperatures are all right throughout the year. *Fenestraria* does not tolerate cold and should not be wintered in an unheated area. Give it the brightest light you can.

The most curious and attractive of the terrarium foliage plants, Ficus pumila quercifolia. *Here it's growing on sphagnum moss in a plastic old-fashioned glass.*

 ## The Miniature Fig Vine
FICUS PUMILA QUERCIFOLIA

Our interest in a plant is sometimes aroused by something unexpected in its appearance rather than by either its beauty or ugliness. When we visualize a family we choose its typical and common members. We expect the daisy family to be daisylike and the phlox family like phlox. And, when we are introduced to a plant that doesn't resemble our preconceived notion, we are astonished and often sceptical. This is particularly true when we find out that some very small unfamiliar plant is related to large common ones. We think of a fig, for example, as a large-leaved fruit tree, a rubber plant, a strangler fig, or the immense banyan. Then, to find a little creeping plant that is so close a relative is something of a shock.

Our exhibits here are really two. The first has been very common in cultivation. It is *Ficus pumila minima*, a creeping, vining plant with heart-shaped leaves, about a ½ inch long, of which one side of the midvein is a bit shorter than the other. With enough warmth and humidity and something to grab on to, this figlet will form a delicate blanket on a wall or pillar just like ivy. The blanket of greenery is neat and hardly ever shows signs of dead leaves. Hung in a basket or pot, it drapes gracefully, with enough strength in the stems to turn upward at the ends. In a terrarium it will cover the back and side panes, creating a natural shadow box.

The second tiny fig is one called by some nurserymen *Ficus quercifolia*. But that is a rather large shrub and, as far as we can find out, the correct name is *F. pumila quercifolia*. For the indoor grower, especially for terrariums, it is a more interesting plant and is also even prettier. The leaves are half the size of *pumila*, and the form is very different. They have the shape of a shield with three lobes and slightly puffy quilting. This vine creeps along with all its leaves looking upward, a shiny green that darkens with age. Given warmth, lots of humidity, and a moist soil it spreads nicely. Fertilizer is unnecessary.

We don't know anybody who has flowered this plant in the house. If they did, it would hardly attract their attention. But we would like to see the fruit which is reported to be yellowish and an inch long—somewhat pear-shaped—just like little figs perhaps. This is quite a production for such a miniature. Also we are told that our plants are in a juvenile stage and that when it grows to maturity in its habitat of the Far East and Australia the leaves become much larger—which brings the fruit more into proportion. It is the same with many jungle vines. They start out in nearly dark conditions on the ground and work their way upward to the light. The leaves then are small and far between. Once they emerge in sunlight, however, they achieve their maximum size and finally fruit. Some other small indoor vines are of this kind. It is why *quercifolia* needs very little light to survive and remains small the way we like it.

The fantastic little leaves of the oak-leaved ficus. Who would dream that this is a relative of the fig tree and the rubber plant?

Geogenanthus undatus *displays its ribbony quilted leaves.* Photo courtesy of Thomas H. Everett.

29 The Seersucker Plant
GEOGENANTHUS UNDATUS

We are not partial to most of the numerous members of the spiderwort family (the *Commelinaceae*) typical of which are the inch plants and other weedy basket trailers that have small pinky, three-petaled flowers. When they are quite small plants, they look pretty with their striped foliage, usually purple beneath, or hairy stems and leaves, but the moment they are big enough for a basket they lose all charm. Their sole right to recommendation is their ease of culture. If you can manage to kill any of these plants, you are a poor indoor gardener indeed. One of the oddities of the family is "Moses in the Cradle," *Rhoeo discolor,* which we almost included in this collection. But the stiff leaves look much better in a Florida garden than indoors, and the little boat with its small white flowers really sounds better than it looks.

Geogenanthus undatus from Peru is another matter. It is called the seersucker plant for good reason, as its remarkable silky appearance is that of a beautiful woven cloth. It has broader leaves than other spiderworts—the proportions are about 2 inches of width to 3 inches of length—and the veins are more prominent. They run parallel to the curved sides in a way that graphically suggests a melon form. Between the veins, in the panes, sections are banded with silvery grey against metallic green and the whole surface is puckered—like seersucker. The backs of the leaves are purplish red and the stems too are reddish.

Geogenanthus does well in Rich Mix with lime and constant moisture. It will do well on the side of a window or anywhere within a foot of the fluorescent tubes. Fertilize with mild solutions of 20–20–20. Keep the temperature above 60° F at all times. It is slow-growing but produces lots of suckers which can be allowed to grow in order to bunch the plant—or detach them and pot them up separately. Supply it with high humidity or mist frequently.

The odd transparent look of the colorful sport gymnocalciums. Note the deep fissures.

30 The Rainbow Cacti
GYMNOCALCIUM SPECIES

In the same way that people think all orchids look like corsage ones and have no idea that you can find plenty of them growing in woods within fifty miles of New York (and most other American cities). the idea that cacti grow only in the deserts of our Southwest is widespread. The reality is that this entirely New World family is common in arid areas all the way from Long Island to southern Argentina. As far as the indoor grower is concerned. some of the South American plants are the better bloomers.

Among the cacti of the southern hemisphere are the gymnocalciums—spherical small plants with bumpy ribs and short sharp spines. In this genus *G. friederickii, mihanovichii,* and others have produced mutants that are so richly colored that they don't seem like cacti at all. Cacti come in many shapes and often have colorful spines or are blanketed in white hairs. but the body of the plant is prevailingly green. The colors of these new plants are no halfway marks but uncompromising oranges. reds. pinks. and yellows. The strains have been continued by selection and hybridization. which has strengthened the colors and the adaptability of the plants.

It is well known that baby cacti grafted on to sections of certain stock plants will grow much faster. Some clever nursery, probably Japanese, got the idea that the small colorful cacti would also sell much better perched on a stalk with all their beauty displayed than sitting on soil half-hidden by a pot rim. Thus the inundation of the rainbow cacti (or, if you prefer another commercial name, cactus bunnies will do). The most successful host has been a cactus with triangular cross section. So now you see these plants everywhere in florist shops, all at the same price, for they are turned out on a production line like machine parts. These sports have been so successful that nurserymen have searched for and introduced plants of other genera which also show some color and are of different shapes—but none compare with the gymnocalciums.

Grow them in their little pots, watering once every two weeks in summer and allowing them to dry out completely in winter except, if the apartment is very dry, providing a bit of moistening once a month. Usually, after you have had the plant awhile, the green lower part begins to branch or suckers develop at the base. These must be cut off. Remember, as long as the stalk does not shrivel the top plant will receive nourishment. So you don't have to be generous to the lower part. That only encourages it to assert its independence.

Gymnocalciums bloom nicely so, with good care and plenty of sun, you will see the quite large red or pink flowers. But this is unnecessary and most people are happy with the bright coloration of the fleshy, spiny bodies.

Plants like *Episcia* 'Cleopatra,' the crestate cacti and succulents and these colorful cacti, which are almost completely lacking in chlorphyll, appeal very much to the public and to "collectors." But real plant people often detest them for the reason that they are not natural, healthy plants, but ones whose display is caused by some abnormality in their genes or an illness due to environmental conditions. There is something, no doubt, artificial about these plants, and their popularity may eventually result in an excess of pathological monsters. We hope not. These exceptions are amusing for a while, but a whole repertory, displacing plants with normal organic development, might be as unpleasant as a collection of plastic ones.

The coarse, hairy leaves of the purple velvet plant give an impression of power. The richness of the coloring is unique. At the same time it's one of the easiest plants to grow in the house.

31 The Purple Velvet Plant
GYNURA AURANTIACA

Since we see chlorophyll, which is so vital to plants, as green in color, how is it possible that some leaves can be brown, silver, red, or purple? Indeed these are exceptions and yet the plants seem to function just as well as those with green foliage. The chlorophyll is there, all right, but masked by pigments of different colors in the cells—whose purpose we know little about.

It might be fun sometime, and rather easy, to make an indoor garden without greenery. You could use *Alternanthera dentata* for red, one of the brown-and-pink or silver-leaved episcias, the black orchid *Ludisia discolor*, banded browns and whites of *Cryptanthus*, the bromeliad, any number of red and silver begonias, *Kalanchoe beharensis*, which is brown, lots of blue or grey succulents, and the white, hairy Old Man cacti, silver *Sinningia leucotricha*, colorful *Coleus*, and the magnificent purple of *Gynura aurantiaca*, the purple velvet plant.

Gynura, a member of the daisy family, comes from Java. There it may grow with a thick stem, branched but erect. In our greenhouse and indoor conditions it is a hanging plant, sending out long streamers of purple stems and leaves from pots or baskets. The leaves are narrow, spear-shaped, and jagged, arranged opposite each other on the thickish hairy stems. With good light it blooms with ½-inch puffs of burnt orange (a daisy without petals) which contrast oddly with the foliage.

Pot gynura in Lean Mix, put it in a sunny window or a favored position under the lights, and keep moist. Fertilize with high-nitrate formula. If you grow it in a basket, let the branches droop, nipping the tips occasionally to make it bush. But, if you want to keep it on the shelf in a pot, it will be necessary to trim and train drastically but carefully. Since leaves are widely spaced, cut the stems right down to the next node and keep clipping the tips until you have a very full tidy compact plant. You will not often see them that way, but it can be done. Properly trained it will take up no more than about 8 inches of shelf space.

We had some hesitation about including so common a plant in this collection. But certainly the color of *Gynura* is unique. We have been told that the bright purple of the hairs disappears in weak light, but those grown under fluorescent lamps have had the richest color of all. We find that keeping it quite wet does not harm. It may flower less easily if constantly moist, but the glow of the leaves and stems is ample compensation. There is nothing quite like it in the plant world.

Gynura's *little flower is just as remarkable as the leaves when seen under magnification. The lower part is dark purple and the explosion at the top a violent burnt orange. It's really a petalless daisy—believe it or not.*

The incredible curry plant (Helichrysum angustifolium). *The grey, powdery leaves emit an aroma of the pure spice mixture. With time the plant grows into a little tree form and will bear small yellow daisy flowers.*

32 The Curry Plant
HELICHRYSUM ANGUSTIFOLIUM

For those who still think that curry is a spice, we must explain that no such thing exists and that the word simply denotes a combination consisting, according to one authority, of allspice, black pepper, red pepper, Cayenne, ginger, cinnamon, cardamon seed, coriander seed, mustard seed, nutmeg, saffron, and turmeric. The exact proportions are a matter of personal preference. There is an odor, however, associated with *packaged* curry powder, which is quite different from the homemade and which, for a long time, we were unable to identify. The ingredients listed on the label never did account for it. Then, one day, we discovered that the addition of garlic powder, not fresh garlic, to the rest of the spices made the difference.

This digression leads up to our experience at a flower show. There we saw exhibited a very fine collection of topiary herbs. Rosemary, myrtle, and others had been grown as shrubs, with a solid mass of twigs and branches creating a rounded shape and zillions of little leaves on the outside. One of these plants attracted us because of its small, very grey, furry leaves. And, like any good lover of herbs, we snitched a leaf, crushed, and smelled it. Packaged curry powder, forsooth? (Not homemade.) It was unmistakable. Thus we discovered the curry plant, which is *Helichrysum angustifolium*, a member of the daisy family. We continue to grow it as one of those herbal curiosities that has no use, but is a delightful snare for every visitor. Smell it, we say. What's your guess?

Small plants can be bought at a modest price from herb nurseries—where else? It likes a Lean Mix with lime and a position where it gets a few hours of sunlight a day or 4 inches under the fluorescent tubes. Keep it just moist—it doesn't like sogginess—and fertilize only once a month with a balanced solution. By trimming it religiously and constantly shaping, you may have a specimen like the one we admired five years or so ago. Cuttings root rather easily. Oh—and if it has enough sun it produces little yellow daisy flowers. A fun plant.

Homalocladium platycladum, *a charming plant in all its distressing disarray.*

33 Tapeworm Plant
HOMALOCLADIUM PLATYCLADUM

This weirdy is also called the ribbon bush and the centipede plant. But that is mild compared to its Latin name, *Homalocladium platycladum,* which is a sort of taxonomist's nightmare and an insult to any self-respecting plant. The "clad" part stands for shoot or branch, the root, "hom," means "in one piece" (as in homogeneous), and "platy" means broad. We wish that botanists in concocting such synthetic names would avoid such horrors. No wonder some people refuse to learn the Latin names. If we admit that we like the plant itself there will be those who, having read our piece on the Hindu rope plant, will probably cry "prejudice." We can understand how the tapeworm plant can be just as much a bore and a weed for some people as it is amusing for us.

Consider that its home is the Solomon Islands, that it belongs to a family, the *Polygonaceae,* hardly renowned for providing floriferous plants for house or garden, and that, at its best, it is a 1-to-2-foot clump of ribbonlike stems with ½-to-¾-inch arrow-shaped leaves coming out of the joints. Imagine yourself in the Solomon Islands and seeing this plant growing among other vegetation. Would you single it out to bring it home and grow it or even dream of cultivating it commercially? Whoever did just that must have possessed second sight, for most of us would have passed it by without a glance, yet it is now a recognized and reasonably popular houseplant.

85

Undoubtedly the popularity is due to its unusual appearance, seen by itself, and the ease with which it can be grown in the house. Its behavior is as odd as its looks. For a long time we had a plant that lost its leaves seasonally, which we attributed to a fungus infection—a sort of grey mold—and lack of light. Indeed, we had relegated it to a kitchen window that didn't get even a scrap of direct sunlight and where it seemed to do very well for most of the year. The mold was real, all right. It formed a grey scum on the leaves which prompty went limp and dropped. It took us months to get rid of the infection. It never occurred to us to read about it in a book.

When we did check up we found out that *Homalocladium* blooms with clusters of greenish flowers plastered in alternate joints and that this generally takes place when the plant is leafless. The seasonal loss of leaves is generally accompanied by a change in the environment. Our moldy homalocladium was probably being overwatered at the wrong season.

Leafless, the plant really displays its oddity to the full, as nothing remains except the stiff, broad, longitudinally striate stems, which are both woebegone and amusing, like green noodles. Then it gradually leafs out again from the old nodes and looks very green and bushy. In the Solomons it grows 4 feet high and the lower parts of the canes are round in cross section. Older plants in the house will also have round stems below. We have never seen the plant bloom and are only mildly curious.

We are too far away from the Solomon Islands to investigate the cause of this plant's curious appearance. But, on the insufficient evidence of analogous situations, we suspect that it grows close to the ocean and in a sandy habitat. Many of our native plants, growing in protected bays and in salt marshes, develop succulent or seaweedy stems that are very much alike. Perhaps *Homalocladium* just crawled in from the sea.

Culture is very easy. A mixture of sand and loam with some compost or straight Lean Mix is perfectly satisfactory. It does prefer to be rather dry in summer and moist in winter. The leaves do not like direct summer sun, so give it a position to the side of the window or a foot or more below the fluorescent lamps. It will flourish in any temperature down to the forties.

A close-up of the ribbon stem and arrow-shaped leaves of the tapeworm plant.

This example of Hoya carnosa compacta *is not as twisted and tortured as the ones you're used to. But it's in bloom and hoya flowers are* always *beautiful.*

34 Hindu Rope Plant

HOYA CARNOSA COMPACTA

We can understand the charm of a weather-beaten and tortured desert plant that, in self-defense, has developed a monstrous shape or reduced itself to a minimum of function. But why anyone should go into ecstasies over the repulsive foliage of the Hindu rope plant—officially *Hoya carnosa compacta*—is beyond us. There is no excuse for this totally formless, twisted string of leaves, which seems to have been created with malice aforethought. Like all hoyas this one has beautiful clusters of fragrant pendent flowers, but most people, believe it or not, buy and grow it entirely because of its foliage.

Hoya carnosa, the wax plant or vine, which is the normal one, is also very popular and for years has been common in variety stores and everywhere else plants are sold. There are a number of variations from the green-leaved type—patternings in white and with red tints on new growth. And there are many other species all originating in Asia and the Philippines. *Carnosa* is generally preferred because of its medium size, slow growth, and very thick decorative leaves. It can be raised in a pot as well as hung in a window where it can trail, or it can be trained on a small trellis. The star-shaped pink flowers with red centers look like cinnamon hard candy, or glass or clear plastic. They are deliciously fragrant and appear in clusters on the end of short thick stalks, which should never be removed from any of the hoyas, because they are capable of producing bloom over and over again.

The Hindu rope plant differs from the normal plants only in the way the leaves are shrunk and curved under like bacon that has been broiled on just one side. Some names in the trade are 'Twisted Rope,' 'Curls,' and 'Green Kurls' (oof!). They're all the same. A variety called 'Mauna Loa' is even trademarked as *H. Lura-Lei.* This one has the vast distinction of gold centers to the leaves. It sells so fast, we hear, that the producers can't keep up with the demand. This proves one thing—that there's profit in odd and curious plants.

Growing hoyas of this type is simple enough. For foliage alone they can stand a good deal of shade, and a position well back from or to the side of a sunny window is sufficient. The soil should be Lean Mix with lime, packed tight, and the plant should never have more root room than its minimum needs. Although confined, drainage must be good and watering takes place only after the soil is well dried out. Fertilize with fish emulsion once every two weeks in summer and once a month in winter.

Hoya takes a while to get used to a new home. It may well be a year or more before it is sufficiently comfortable to begin flowers. Good sunlight encourages bloom and strengthens the color of the blossoms. Flowering sometimes takes place chronically, both in summer and winter, once the plants start to perform. However, where the window light is poor most of the year, you can only expect bloom between spring and fall. Each peduncle or stalk needs a considerable rest before it performs again, though blossoms may develop in the meanwhile on new growth.

It is interesting to flower this variation of hoya because the contrast between the neat, lovely flowers and the contorted foliage is so curious. Lovers of this plant can look forward, however, to the day when hybridizers succeed in distorting the flower to conform with the rest of the plant. Hallelujah.

The waxy variegated foliage of Hoya carnosa *makes it a popular favorite.*

No, not glass flowers but those of Hoya bella. Bella *means beautiful, and so they are—perfumed too.*

The pink splashes on the leaves of Hypoestes sanguinolenta *have earned it the common name of polka dot plant.*

35 The Polka Dot Plant
HYPOESTES SANGUINOLENTA

The polka dot plant comes by its common name honestly and, considering how much chance plays a role, luckily. For it might well have been saddled with something like the measles plant. Evenly distributed over these normal green leaves are small, clear pink, almost round spots. The effect is cheerful and not a bit like so many of the spotty-leaved plants—aucubas, for instance—which look as if they were just some other victims of the painters on a redecorating job.

This is another plant from Madagascar but not the usual succulent kind. Its one-and-a-half-to-two-inch leaves are thin, soft, and hairy, and both in this respect and in its flowers it resembles more a member of the mint than the acanthus family to which it belongs and which supplies us with so many other beautiful blooming houseplants.

Hypoestes becomes shrubby with age and will grow a couple of feet high. Recently 1-foot specimens, with rather thick, very hairy, stems, have been available at garden centers. This is a juvenile condition and evidence that it has been forced into very rapid growth. Without special care such plants deteriorate rapidly in the house. That shouldn't happen, for the polka dot plant normally is ridiculously easy to grow. Cuttings should be made right away and simply stuck into constantly moist Lean

Mix. They will root in a week and insure you against loss. The cuttings will grow with greener stems in the relatively low humidity of the house but will be just as pretty.

Once established *Hypoestes* is nearly foolproof, requiring only average house temperatures—60° or higher—Lean Mix with lime, constant moisture, and balanced fertilizer occasionally. The only thing you have to watch is its rapid growth. Before you know it the stems are too long and, being on the weak side, begin to pull the plant over. The cure is to trim constantly. This growth habit also means that it is not very durable. Six to eight months of charm is all you can expect. But cuttings root so easily and grow so fast that you can have a constant succession of plants coming on. Don't worry about flowers. They are spikes of lavender and not worth much.

A baby boojum tree—the size for the house—has a pathetic appearance like a despairing sea creature. But, though it takes a terrible beating in the desert, it has the secret of survival.

36 The Boojum Tree
IDRIA COLUMNARIS

Baja California turned up constantly in the news a few years back. This long, narrow spit of land had only a settlement or two on the southern tip and only the most primitive track for a road down from the state of California. The intervening space was hotter and drier than anywhere else on the continent except, perhaps, Death Valley. It became a major sporting challenge to drive the length of the peninsula and a literary challenge to produce a book about it. There wasn't really that much to write about it except to report on breakdowns, lizards, iguanas, and boojum trees.

The boojum tree was a sensation. Other treelike forms in the desert were just tall cacti, but here was a real tree which had made the transition to a life without water. To accomplish this feat it became a very odd-looking object. When, after a long period of drought it was treated to some rain it looked like a tall inverted carrot—thirty feet or more high. The trunk was spiny and had very short branches at the top which leafed out and bore clusters of yellow flowers. After this productive burst no more rain would occur for a long time—sometimes measured in years. Gradually the pulpy trunk lost its moisture, the carrot came to look more like a spiny asparagus as the whole plant shrank and, in its anguish, the poor thing leaned over like a very tired, overcooked asparagus indeed. This impressed the naturalists no end.

So the boojum tree is a first-class curiosity and anyone who enjoys the odd and curious should have one. Well, you can. Whether the nurseries rooted sections or are enjoying a crop from seed we know not. but boojums are now available from cactus and succulent nurseries. Don't expect anything very elegant. It will come in anything from a 6-inch pot to a 15-inch tub (or bigger) as a mere irregular cone covered with 2-or-3-inch-long branches looking dead as doornails. But it is unmistakably boojum.

Take this gem and place it in your sunniest location and moisten it occasionally during the summer months. It will green out nicely. This is somewhat unfortunate since it looks much less interesting alive than dead. But the advantage is that it will grow and. in fact. rather rapidly. everything considered. During the winter you can leave it safely without water at all. If it shrivels give it a modest drink—on a sunny day. Young plants. because the soil in the pot is shallow. should receive more moisture than older specimens. If you have to move it eventually to a larger pot—it has extensive roots—give it Cactus and Succulent Mix. Fertilizer is wasted on it.

These boojum trees in Baja California are in their prime, having recently received some rain. Soon they will lose their leaves and wait patiently for the next downpour which may be a year or more away. Photo courtesy of Thomas H. Everett.

The magnificent velvet leaves of Kalanchoë beharensis.

37 The Velvet Leaf Plant
KALANCHOE BEHARENSIS

The velvet leaf plant comes from the mysterious island of Madagascar. Madagascar is mysterious because, though the third largest island in the world, it is very little known to most of us. However we have heard of the lemurs and other strange animals, as well as equally curious plants, that are peculiar to this region, isolated for a long time from outside influences.

A number of popular kalanchoës originated on this island. They have tube flowers, some pretty, some dull, and succulent leaves often sprouting young plants along their edges, which drop to the ground and root immediately. They are somewhat weedy plants and short-lived but are easily replaced. *K. beharensis* looks very different at first sight, but those who know the larger species often seen in Florida recognize a similarity in the shape of the leaves.

Even when only 1½ feet high it has a pulpy stem, like that of a sumac, 1½ inches thick, and a few leaves are already at least a foot long. They aren't real. Arrowhead-shaped, they look for all the world as if made of cardboard covered with a film of brown flocking twisted by the action of a drip from the ceiling. They stand straight out, are wavy along the edges, and folded somewhat down the middle. The underside is clear grey.

The feel of this leaf is equally extraordinary. It is stiff, dry, and brittle. Bend it and it breaks like a soda cracker. Rub your finger over the pile. It is short and stiff like a kind of cloth formerly used to upholster cars and which proved so irritating to a bare elbow on the door rest.

As the velvet leaf plant grows—a satisfyingly slow process—the leaves on the lower parts dry up and drop off leaving a rosette or cluster of new leaves at the top. Once we grew a specimen in a good-sized tub to a height of 8 feet—which proved it was alive. At that point, being more than we could handle, we offered it to a botanical garden. Alas, there were no takers. One day we came home and found that the top weight had proved too much for it and it had broken in two. We are sorry we let it go at that. We didn't know at the time that those dry leaves were capable of rooting and producing new plants, just like an African violet.

The leaves of the velvet leaf plant are a particular delight to a child. We often speak of the velvety leaves on plants—episcias, some aroids, etc. But this is one of the few plants that provide a real thrill to the touch. Besides, in spite of its oddity, it is a noble sight when about 3 feet tall.

Grow *K. beharensis* in a 12-inch pot or a larger tub packed with Lean Mix with lime. Watered once a week in summer and once every two weeks in winter, it will do well in reflected light from a window, on a sun porch, or anywhere there is moderate illumination. Don't be misled by its dry appearance, which suggests a full sunny position. It can tolerate it but is almost equally happy in shade. Fertilizer is hardly necessary at all, but the plant may benefit from balanced formula every few months. A slow grower, it will last several years with care. So don't rush it by overwatering or overfeeding. It does not need high humidity.

Make a slash from the edge toward the center of one of the lower leaves and plantlets will sprout all along the two edges. These can be cut free and planted up. Or cut a lower leaf off while still healthy and lay all or part of it on moist mix. Pin it down on the surface with hairpins. A humid atmosphere at this stage aids root development.

Recently, smaller relatives with smaller leaves but sufficiently velvety have appeared in numbers on the market. Probably this is *Kalanchoë velutina* or *K.* 'Roseleaf.' For those who don't have the space, this makes a fine substitute and a foolproof plant to grow. Pieces of leaf cut here and there with scissors and pinned to moist mix sprout into little plants in no time.

Sometimes K. beharensis *develops a more varied shape. The surface of the leaf is hard-hairy to the touch.*

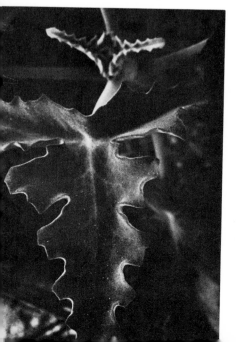

Kalanchoë 'Roseleaf,' *showing the hard, remarkably hairy leaves.*

This waxy 4-inch-long drooping lily is the national flower of Chile. It's a stunner for the house. Photo courtesy of Bernard Alfieri.

38 Lily Vine
LAPAGERIA ROSEA

A friend who recently returned from Chile told us that she just couldn't understand why all the shopwindows and many homes displayed red plastic flowers so prominently—until she happened to touch one and discovered, with a shock, that they were real. The flower in question forms a 4-inch-long, 6-petaled pendent lily of heavy, waxy substance, colored lacquer red, pink, white, or white with pink spots. No one who has ever seen it will forget it.

Well, there is good reason for its being shown so freely in Chile, for it is the national flower. It is *Lapageria rosea,* named for Napoleon Bonaparte's first wife, Josephine de la Pagerie, who grew it in the greenhouse of Malmaison, near Paris. It is a vigorous vine which, when well grown as you may see it, for instance, at Logee's Greenhouses in Connecticut, is strung with blooms for most of the year.

Lapageria does belong to the lily family and, if you compare the leaves with those of the genus *Smilax* which grows in our woods, the plants seem almost identical. Isn't it strange that this deep-rooted spiny weed with dull-colored small leaves, which produces with us clusters of tiny greenish flowers, should, in the southern hemisphere, burst into such incredible beauty? Grown in a pot we have had vines not more than a couple of feet long, attached to a small trellis and looking totally undecorative, bloom with immense long-lasting gorgeous flowers. They stay on for weeks.

This justly famous plant has only recently been much cultivated in the United States. The difficulty has been in propagating it, and for years experiments were carried out with all kinds of methods. There were also two other problems. It cannot stand much root disturbance and can't be divided. Finally, it is so very acid loving that it is allergic to lime in even minute quantities. It should be added, in order to caution you thoroughly, that it prefers coolth, hence does better on the West Coast and in England than in the warm homes of our East.

Plants, which are not cheap, should be bought and carefully checked for mite infestation to which they are subject. Wash leaves thoroughly and hang a No-Pest Strip nearby if you find any evidence. Grow in moderate sun in a humus-rich acid soil (not soilless mix) and water well during growth in spring and summer and very little in winter. Do not fertilize more than once every couple of months and then only during the growing season and with a 30–10–10 solution. If leaves look poorly or drop, add some Sequestrene (chelated iron) to the soil.

Lapageria wants plenty of room for roaming roots. Provide, therefore, a minimum 10-inch pot or a small tub. In winter try to keep it at 50° F and allow to nearly dry out each time before watering lightly. This is a "fits and starts" plant. But once it has established itself, it will grow into a fairly large vine that must be wrapped around some kind of trellis.

Lapageria is a magnificent plant and a showstopper, but only those willing to devote time and effort to it should make the attempt of growing it indoors.

Lithops olivacea *growing among stone chips. From stand-up viewing height they are lost to sight in this environment. And then they bloom with large and brightly colored flowers.* Photo courtesy of Bernard Alfieri.

39 The Living Stones
LITHOPS SP.

A great many of our most unusual plants come from South Africa because their adaptation to a desert environment is even more drastic and varied there than in our American deserts. Among the succulents, especially of the family *Aizoaceae,* are numerous plants that look so much like stones that for most of the year they are difficult to tell apart from real ones. Among these the most popular as houseplants are the *Lithops,* which may be considered the champs at simplification. It is as if they had deprived themselves of nearly all the normal growth habits of a plant and retreated into a quiescent state, harboring their resources, without much hope, except at long intervals, of receiving any moisture or nourishment at all. And then, for a short moment each year, they produce their large flowers and spread their seeds. They are little plants which, sunken in the burning sand and beaten by a pitiless sun by day, suffer a severe drop in temperature at night. To withstand such natural onslaughts, they have resorted to a minimum of activity.

This curious mode of life is in itself no recommendation, but amateurs are charmed by the great variety of colors and markings on these plants and the astonishing display of their flowers. The only real difficulties in growing them are in seeing that they get enough sunlight and are, in other respects, treated far worse than we would like. More lithops are killed by kindness than anything else, for deprivation is what they expect and thrive on. It has been found that cacti often benefit from

This little fellow looks as if the doctor had just removed the stitches following an operation. His color happens to be pink. Its label says Lithops julii.

Lithops leslei var. hornii *is in the process of giving birth to a new leaf.*

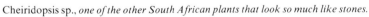

Cheiridopsis sp., *one of the other South African plants that look so much like stones.*

milder conditions than their habitats. Similar attempts with lithops are deadly.

The body of a lithops plant before flowering is like a pair of half-round smooth stones pressed together with a shallow cleft running between. Some species in the early stages of growth do not even have that and are totally smooth and nearly round. The diameter ranges from ½ inch to rare giants of 2 inches. At most they stick ½ inch above the soil. The bud appears in the cleft, which spreads to accommodate the flower stalk and bursts open. The flower covers an area four or more times that of the body. The blooming is preceded by the only possibly moist period of the year. After that the plant enters a period of total dryness. The two stones start to shrivel and flatten. Markings and slight depressions appear on the surface. The smooth skin—whitish, grey, tan, or reddish—is squiggled with darker lines. Eventually the two sides are so reduced that they are no more than a skin. At this point the new growth, identical with the old, begins to emerge, finally splitting the covering and growing the following summer into a replacement.

Lithops signals its need for water by its own activity. When it starts to grow it should be watered very gently and allowed to dry in between. The period is usually spring to fall. From fall to spring no water whatsoever should be given, although a misting once very couple of weeks will simulate a desert dew. Use a very sandy or Lean Mix with perfect drainage and always pot rather big to give plenty of room for roots. For instance, three or four of these little plants should be in a 4-inch pot—preferably of clay. Once a year, during the growth period, they can be watered with a very mild solution of fish emulsion.

The humidity demands are, of course, nil or nearly so. We always forget that even in the driest desert air the sudden drop of temperature at night causes some slight moisture to be attracted to the plant—hence the misting. Bright sunlight or its equivalent they must have. If possible, place them on the windowsill during the summer months, where they receive full light and good heat. This is one reason for the large pots. Shallow pots and a small amount of soil will overheat and damage the roots.

When buying lithops, of which there are very many species and variations, consult the nurseryman about the types best for growing indoors without maximum light. Many amateurs do grow them successfully indoors. We have had only short experience growing them under fluorescent light, but so far they have done very well. A considerable collection of these extraordinary plants can be grown in an area no bigger than a standard card table.

One of the most beautiful leaves in the world—Ludisia discolor. *The background is deep brown black and the veining is a rich red orange. The other plant is* Selaginella uncinata, *the peacock selaginella, see page 141.*

40 The Black Leaf Orchid
LUDISIA DISCOLOR VAR. DAWSONIANA

Out of bloom the orchids are certainly among the ugly ducklings of the plant world. A greenhouse full of orchid greenery consists of masses of large donkey ears, occasional quill shapes, and some grassy effects. Yet this family is so enormous that there are exceptions to every rule. There is in fact a large group of terrestrial orchids, bearing spikes of relatively small flowers, that display creeping whorls of unusually beautiful leaves. They grow in moist woods in many parts of the world and in this country are represented by the goodyeras, commonly called rattlesnake plantains. If, walking in oak woods, you see clusters of leaf rosettes, green with distinct checkerboard white veining, those are the leaves of the goodyeras. In July-August each rosette throws up a spike with little white flowers.

In the Himalaya region there are similar plants. And, all through Southeast Asia and the Indies, various species can be found with velvety green or bronzy leaves, sometimes even dark red, with gold or coppery veinings. Most unusual of all is *Ludisia discolor,* especially the variety *Dawsoniana.* The leaves of this superb plant are very nearly black, velvety, and covered with a complex network of veining which is brilliant reddish copper in color. In spring it blooms with spikes a foot or more tall—the flowers white, of modest size, and curiously twisted. But it is the leaves that count, and a well-grown mass of them is breathtaking.

A foolproof way of growing these plants is the following. Let's presume that you have bought a pot, containing two or three stems with a whorl of leaves at the tip. Put an inch of gravel in the bottom of a rectangular or round glass terrarium. Cover with a 3- or 4-inch layer of woods moss or sheet moss. Take the plant out of the pot, disturbing the roots as little as possible, and plant it at an angle in the moss on one side of the terrarium so that the stems lie on the moss with the leaves facing up. Moisten the moss with high-nitrogen solution (30–10–10) and enough liquid to see just a thin film on the bottom of the gravel. Put a transparent cover on the terrarium and leave open about an inch at one end.

In a few weeks the stems will have sent out beautiful orange hairy roots and will start to crawl across the surface of the moss. The plant can be left there until too big for the terrarium. A good planting on the surrounding moss would be *Selaginella uncinata,* the blue kind, and *Sinningia pusilla.* When the plant has grown too big, sections of the very thick stems can be cut and laid in similar conditions on moss. These will root and put up leaves in due time, though considerable patience is required.

As you can see, ludisia requires high humidity. Also the temperature should not drop below 60° F, and there must be no sogginess of the medium. Overwatering kills it. Moistness and good aeration of the moss or soil are musts. As these are very acid plants, they should always be fertilized with fish emulsion or 30–10–10 formula.

Ludisias of the best quality are moderately scarce. Check the catalogs of orchid nurseries and importers. Once you have a plant it can last and multiply forever.

Ludisia with flower spike.

Barbados holly—holly foliage, exquisite pink flowers—an exciting houseplant.

Malpighia's complicated flower seen close up.

41 Who's the Mimic?

MALPIGHIA COCCIGERA

On the island of Grand Bahama there are three interesting and curiously interrelated plants. Two are orchids—*Oncidium bahamense* and *Oncidium lucayanum.* The other is the familiar *Malpighia coccigera,* or Barbados holly. Malpighia is an excellent and attractive houseplant. Oncidiums are popular too. They are spray orchids, predominantly yellow in color but with a number of species with pink flowers like malpighia.

Malpighia coccigera is a small shrub with ½-inch leaves of true holly shape, spines and all. The pink flowers, about an inch across, are quite unusual. The center is a bumpy round mass consisting of the calyx and nectaries located in the sepals. The petals are five, ruffled-round in outline and connected to the center by very narrow stalks. One of the five petals is less rounded, somewhat larger, and possesses a thicker stalk. There is a considerable superficial resemblance between this flower and those of the oncidiums.

Now the plot thickens. Oncidiums of different species can usually be crossed or hybridized rather easily by the hand of man. Natural hybrids are also a frequent occurrence in the Caribbean islands between the many different oncidium species that often grow close together. A short time ago the curiosity of scientists was aroused by the fact that large colonies of our two Grand Bahaman species failed to interbreed. A study group was sent there to find out why.

The first thing observed was that *O. bahamense* was visited exclusively by female bees, which collect food. *O. lucayanum* opened only at a time when the male bees were active. This solved the main problem but raised some others. Why did the female bees go to collect food at a flower which had none to offer? And why did the male bees, who do not collect food, visit the other orchid?

The scientists suspected that there was some relationship between the malpighia flower, which does contain nectar, and *O. bahamense,* which does not. Our learned detectives know that the eyes of bees are sensitive to ultraviolet light rather than the parts of the spectrum that are visible to us. When they took ultraviolet photographs of malpighia flowers and those of *Oncidium bahamense* the pictures showed a similar pattern—a lobed round area in the center of the flower and a fleshy stem connecting it to the stigmatic and stamen areas.

The assumption is that what the female bee saw in both flowers was the same landing place, the same stem to clutch with its claws while it fed, and the same nectaries. In other words, the orchid had accomplished the amazing trick of evolving a central area of its flower that presented a malpighialike ultraviolet image to the bee. And, whereas the malpighia offered food, the orchid only made believe that it was equally bountiful.

When ultraviolet photos were taken of the other orchid, *Oncidium lucayanum,* the image was quite different. The center of the flower looked like the body of an insect and the upper part like two wings. The principal business of the male bee is protecting his territory. When this orchid opened he "saw" an intruder and dive-bombed the flower.

Thus the orchids had fooled both the female and male bees in order to accomplish cross-pollination. The female bee would never visit the other orchid no matter when it opened because it gave no promise of food. The male bee would never dive-bomb *O. bahamense* because it did not look like an intruder. Hence the two orchids would never be mated—and our scientists went home to write the solution of their plant detective story.

Malpighia is a special favorite of bonsai amateurs who dwarf it. The woody habit, the many twigs, the small holly leaves, and the silky pink flowers make it a most sought-after subject. As a general houseplant it is a charmer and, when well grown, is literally covered with flowers. Years ago we saw it for the first time in the window of, believe it or not, a swank New York bakery. There was a plant a good 18 inches across— virtually a pinky mist. We have never since seen one so perfectly grown. At the time we did not know it at all and hastened, after reaching home, to our books and an identification.

Malpighia likes our Lean Mix with a double dose of lime chips, mimicking its habitat, which is near the seashore in sandy soil, where there is a good sprinkling of small seashells mixed with the earth. Its main problem is getting established. It has a way of sulking for as much as six months before beginning to grow. And during that time it must be watered very carefully, and rather sparingly. But once it starts to send out branches and leaves it can be kept evenly moist—that is, as long as temperatures are over 60° F. Being a low plant, accustomed to living beneath other vegetation, it does not require very much light. An east window or a place 15 inches below the tubes will bring it into bloom in due time. Spring is its normal flowering period but, under fluorescent lights, it may bloom chronically throughout the year. To insure bloom, temperatures must be over 70°, as it usually does not set buds at lower ranges. The buds are cute, by the way—little tiny beads of pink which one never expects to produce a flower an inch across. Fertilize only once every couple of weeks in summer with a balanced formula. In winter cut to once a month. Malpighia will survive all right in a dry atmosphere but is a more reliable performer if the humidity is over 50 percent— remember, the air can get awfully damp at the seashore.

A couple of pansy orchids seem to fly above the foliage. Photo courtesy of Donald Richardson.

42 The Giant Pansy
MILTONIA VEXILLARIA HYBRIDS

If you have never seen one of the great hybrid pansy orchids in bloom—and most people have not—you are in for a real shock when you come across it at an orchid nursery or spring flower show. The plants are often quite small, while the flowers are as much as 5 inches in diameter, with three or more in a spray. The brilliant colors and clear zonings make them appear even bigger than they are. With all the petals arranged on the same plane, they have little resemblance to other orchids and are more like giant pansies—which is what people are likely to take them for at first sight. Breathtaking is the only word for it. Happily, with a little extra care, these marvelous flowering plants can now be grown indoors either on a windowsill or under lights.

Miltonia is a small genus from Brazil and Colombia with some species growing as far north as Costa Rica. *M. vexillaria* is the species that has been used most in hybridization, and crosses of this parent with others have resulted in the largest and most brilliant blooms. These hybrids come in every color from white through pink to blood red along with yellow splotchings. Combinations of color are infinite, and every hybrid displays a different design. There is no other orchid that has quite this cool clarity of color and clear zoning as if a master artist had used his imagination to create them.

The flattened pseudobulbs of these miltonias are only a few inches tall with long narrow leaves growing from the tips. The blooming stalks appearing from the base of the pseudobulb, one on each side, are arching and bear up to six flowers. When there are several new pseudobulbs in a pot, there may be numerous sprays of flowers and a tremendous display. Alas, a week is as much as you can expect from the single flowers, although two weeks is not uncommon. The advantage of a pot with several pseudobulbs is that the show can last for two months or more in spring.

We have seen an incredible plant win best of show in an important competition—a plant in a 3-inch pot with two or three pseudobulbs and a single spray bearing four of these enormous flowers, each one bigger than the pot and completely hiding it, the pseudobulbs, and the rather thin zigzag stem.

Allow no more than an inch of space around the roots of miltonias—they like it tight. Pot up in fine fir bark with some perlite added. Fill the bottom of the pot with mix, set the Miltonia upright, and stuff mix in around the roots, using a potting stick to lever the mix inward toward the roots until the plant is firm and the level of the mix is just up to the bottom of the pseudobulbs. Do this once a year without fail, in late spring after flowering, or in early fall. Allow the mix to dry out between waterings but then water thoroughly and, during active growth, use a high-nitrate solution (30–10–10) about one-quarter strength. Roots burn easily and decayed compost produces rot.

Temperatures at night should be as near 60° as possible and not over 80° at any time for long periods. A cellar, an air-conditioned apartment with humidifier, or an airy sun porch or window with an east or west exposure are all satisfactory. Miltonias require relatively little light and are more like the moth orchids in this respect. Therefore they do well under artificial light but require a fair amount of moving air—hence a fan—and high humidity, over 50 percent. In case of leaf browning use a fungicide dip recommended as effective against damping-off.

If you are buying your first pansy orchid, ask the nurseryman for a *M. vexillaria* hybrid which is as adaptable as possible. Say that you are growing indoors. With experience and some reading, you will learn to pick your own. Since good plants of these hybrids are quite expensive, count on giving it maximum attention.

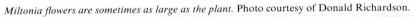

Miltonia flowers are sometimes as large as the plant. Photo courtesy of Donald Richardson.

The sensitive plant being tested. As soon as the leaf is touched, the leaflets will fold and the whole leaf will assume a vertical position. After a while it gets tired of being vertical and tries horizontal·again.
Photo courtesy of Thomas H. Everett.

43 The Sensitive Plant
MIMOSA PUDICA

I do not come to celebrate the sensitive plant but to warn you. Certainly none of the odd ones attracts more instant attention. For good reason. Plenty of plants fold their leaves at night, some drop them or raise them and others, like fire fern, are continuously semaphoring, but none of these can compare with good old *Mimosa Pudica* for immediate action. Touch a leaf and it folds up and drops down from the elbow. Adults are as fascinated as children. It's a pretty, small, sprawling plant and generally quite inoffensive. The leaves, with numerous segments, and the stems are delicate.

Almost everyone knows of this plant, but not everybody has grown it. Those who have must treat it and enjoy it for its novelty, since it doesn't usually last long enough to be anything else. The awful truth is that it may be a fine plant for a hot, dry, sunny life in Brazil, whence it comes, but doesn't adapt well at all to indoor growing. The life is short and not necessarily merry in most cases.

We have another bone to pick with this plant. Everyone who sees a plant in our home with multi-leaflet leaves, usually of the pea family, asks whether it isn't a sensitive plant or a mimosa. And we have to go through a whole rigmarole of explanation time and again.

The sensitive plant is indeed a mimosa. Almost all other plants that look like it are not. The genus is not a big one. The florist "mimosas," for instance, are acacias from Australia. There are innumerable tropical trees and shrubs with such leaves and these belong to various genera.

It is a creeping briar which develops thin, ground-hugging, spiny branches and blooms with a lavender sphere of small flowers. Down South there are a number of wild plants very much like it, but none of these has been smart enough to learn the touch trick.

In the small pot in which it is usually bought, the sensitive plant seems to wear itself out and to collapse after a short time for no apparent reason. It may be more than normally sensitive to the change from greenhouse humidity and light to the inferior conditions in most homes. Moved to a broad shallow pot it has a chance to creep and root, causing it to last somewhat longer. Pruning will encourage it to branch. Luckily cuttings root easily in moist Lean Mix, so you can have more plants coming along as the old one nears the end of its rope. Keep it in full sunlight, water well, and fertilize rarely. Count on a short life but, hopefully, a merry one for this tricky fellow.

Give it some sunshine and Mimosa pudica *will bloom prettily.* Photo courtesy of Thomas H. Everett.

The featheriest of ferns—Nephrolepis exaltata var. Norwoodii. A much easier houseplant than one would expect and than most of the more delicate tropical ferns.

44 The Feathery Ferns
NEPHROLEPIS EXALTATA VAR. NORWOODII

Why do some related plants mutate more than others? We just don't know. Change of weather or water supply or a marginal situation in the group environment may cause it. Some genera mutate with a specific frequency whatever the apparent circumstances.

What is a mutation? Well, just a recognizable change in the structure or appearance of a plant. In nature the vast majority of such new plants die out quickly due to the loss of some characteristic essential to survival. But when they occur in nurseries and are considered an improvement in appearance, they are propagated for the trade. That is how many new interesting house plants are born.

Among ferns for the house, two, the Bostons and the table ferns, are mutable to a high degree. The original species, parent of the Boston ferns, was *Nephrolepis exaltata,* a coarse plant with five-foot leaves found throughout the tropical world. From cultivated plants of this giant, a mutant was selected many years ago and became famous as the Boston fern—*N. exaltata* var. *Bostoniensis.* It is a more graceful, drooping plant and was a great porch fern in grandma's time. Wherever this plant has been grown in large numbers, new mutations have occurred and they are now so numerous that nurserymen have as hard a job finding new names for them as the owners of racing stables have inventing names for their foals.

108

The latest of these variations is that awful 'Fluffy Ruffles,' which seems to be the label for any very brittle, stiff, erect medium-size fern that propagates like a weed. In an entirely different class are those called 'Norwoodii' and 'Whitmanii,' of which we prefer the former. These have the most finely divided leaves of all the ferns. A well-grown plant of 'Norwoodii' looks like green foam and is far more delicate than the finest lace. When it is allowed to "take off" in a very humid warm terrarium, we have seen it develop leaves that consist of several layers of pure gossamer which completely filled the vessel.

Some years ago 'Norwoodii' and other fine-leaved Boston ferns were common in florist shops, but lately they have been hard to find. However, the nurseries have them. You can start with a small plant, since it grows quite rapidly, spreading by means of threadlike green rhizomes. Short rhizomes root close to the parent plant, while others wave around in the air reaching out for new territories to conquer. As your plant grows you can move it progressively to larger pots filled with Rich Mix with lots of lime. Water constantly. Although so delicate in appearance it can tolerate a fair amount of dryness, but some dead leaves are an almost inevitable result. We have been successful in growing it well in an area of our home that has very low humidity. This adaptability gives 'Norwoodii' a very great advantage over many of the tropical ferns sold as suitable for indoor growing.

Eventually your best size pot is a plastic 7-inch azalea type. If happy, the plant will be a pile of greenery almost a foot high and hanging down evenly around the edges of the pot. Leaves become so intermingled that it is difficult to differentiate them. If you have to break up the plant, just divide it into sections of leaf and root. You will have a dozen plants at least from a 7-inch pot.

The 'Norwoodiis' grown in the dry air of our living room originally lived in a lathhouse in Florida. Now they do beautifully under two 24-inch fluorescent tubes. We keep the fern constantly moist and fertilize with a balanced formula along with our other plants. The temperature is maintained at over 60°. Below that level, growth tends to stop and rot to set in. But most homes remain above that temperature in winter. This is one of the marvels of the plant world and a joyful decoration for the house.

Don't attempt to count the leaflets on a fine-leaved Boston fern. They're innumerable.

45 The Bead Plant
NERTERA DEPRESSA

Whereas *Senecio rowleyanus,* the bead vine, is a true succulent with hanging strands of beadlike leaves, *Nertera depressa* (see color section) derives its name from its prolific production of beadlike bright orange berries. It is neither nervous nor depressed, nor a combination of both but simply a shade-loving, matted, small ground plant with insignificant leaves and flowers. However, none of our other creeping tropical houseplants fruit like this one. About ¼ inch across, they provide superdecoration in a small space.

The plant is listed as coming from South America, New Zealand, and Tasmania. Hard to believe, unless Thor Heyerdahl had a hand in it. The tiny leaves are paired and orbicular, making a solid green mat when the plant is in healthy growth. We've been told that it's used as a ground cover on the West Coast.

Grow it in a small pot in a mixture of half sphagnum moss and half sand or perlite. Give reflected light or a position on the side of the light garden. Keep moist but not wet. Seed is available from Park's. Plants from McComb's Greenhouses.

Fire fern—the totally red color of the delicate leaves and the airiness of the whole plant make this a cherished houseplant. The movement of the leaflets is the bonus.

46 Fire Fern
OXALIS HEDYSAROIDES RUBRA

Except that the leaves are red throughout, fire fern really could be mistaken for one of the maidenhair ferns. It is a delightful, colorful, airy plant, which too few indoor growers know and which always attracts attention when it is displayed. Nevertheless it would not find a place in this collection if it were not for its remarkable calisthenics. In the Caribbean islands where it is popular, this trick is recognized as a major attraction of the plant, but most northern growers have never observed it.

Since it belongs to the oxalis family, we expect the leaves to close at night. Most of them have three leaflets, much like three-leaved clover, each of which folds down the center when it goes to sleep. Fire fern works it differently. For one thing the leaves are more separate, each with its short stem, and it doesn't fold. But if you watch the plant on some days, especially when it is feeling frisky, which is usually during hot spells, you will see a motion in the individual leaflets. Watch very closely and suddenly—you will believe that it is an optical illusion—a leaflet will move from the vertical to the horizontal and another, in a different part of the plant, from horizontal to vertical. The rest of the leaf is not affected. Soon you will notice that this quick movement is going on all over the plant at irregular intervals—some leaves going up and others down. It's really something.

This plant performer puts on another show that is even more spectacular but that does not always happen, even under the same circumstances. One day we had to move a largish plant around a good deal and, in doing so, disarranged the branches. After it had been placed in its final position it remained perfectly quiet for several minutes. Then the entire plant suddenly shivered violently and all the branches and leaves changed back to their old positions from which they had been disarranged. The motion stopped as quickly as it began. Many plants do

111

The unusual shape and arrangement of fire fern's leaves. Every leaf consists of three segments, each provided with its own stem.

this because of branches snapping back after being pushed out of alignment. But we have never seen a whole plant do it all at once. We have seen it do the same thing on other occasions when it has been disturbed.

These motions are not visible at all times, and we have not been able to establish exactly under what conditions they take place. We wish we could find out, as we could then create them artificially and make the plant perform for our friends. It is an annoyance to describe so amusing a trick and have the plant fail when on display. Talking to it doesn't work. Nevertheless we are sure you will notice it one of these days.

Fire fern is in more demand than supply because nurserymen find it a rather difficult plant to handle in the greenhouse. We suspect that this is because of the high humidity and the tendency to slosh water on a plant which has every appearance of requiring it. Although they look so delicate, they like neither the humidity nor much water. Rather dry between waterings is, for a change, a really true precaution. And it can tolerate your dry living room very well. It took us a long time to discover that fire fern abominates wet soil. Moderate light is all it needs, although the redness of the leaves is greater under partial sun. Grow it in Rich Mix at the side of a window or at the end of a fluorescent tube. With care it can grow into a fine, graceful specimen, with whippy branches that climb vertically from a solid short trunk. It rarely grows over 15 inches.

To propagate take 3-inch cuttings from branch ends and root in slightly moist vermiculite in an *uncovered* container. Excess moisture will inhibit rooting and lead to rot. The small-rooted cuttings with their ball of red foliage are particularly endearing. The yellow flowers, small and sparse, appear occasionally.

The remarkable gold-veined leaves of Oxalis martiana aureo-reticulata. *Each segment folds up at night.*

47 The Gold-Veined Plant
OXALIS MARTIANA AUREO-RETICULATA

Long before the miracle plants were introduced from the tropics the oxalis was a popular houseplant because it was one of the few that bloomed profusely and easily indoors. There are two kinds—those with normal fibrous roots and the others with bulblets. It is the latter which are the most floriferous. All of them possess leaves like three-leaf clovers and pretty, simple flowers in white, yellow, pink, or red. They are a staple of the plant catalogs. But no one, of course, tells the buyer that after a spate of blooming they go dormant, must be put aside, and that it may be months before signs of life appear again. For the average grower in the house, dormancy is a great nuisance. We don't mind it out-of-doors since our gardens are dormant anyway in winter. But indoors we expect our plants to keep going. The dormant houseplant is, therefore, usually discarded as dead.

There are just two of the bulbous oxalis we know that do not indulge in dormancy indoors. Neither has been a standard houseplant in the past. The reason appears to be that their flowers are not as large as the successful commercial varieties. This is compensated for, however, by unusually beautiful foliage patterns and their ability to stay green and blooming throughout the year. In fact neither of these plants has a blooming season.

Oxalis regnellii, which has small white flowers and triangular leaflets, is a plant you should get to know because it is as foolproof as any in the

113

repertory. But *Oxalis martiana aureo-reticulata* is far more spectacular, and only a bit more difficult to grow. *Aureo-reticulata* means gold-veined. The three bright green leaflets on each pink leaf stalk are more brilliantly veined than any others in the plant kingdom. It's some eye stopper. The flowers, produced in moderate numbers, are small and dark pink.

A single bulblet, about the size of a matchhead, is sufficient to start with. Plant in Rich Mix with lime, water plentifully, and maintain temperature over 60° F. Fertilized with fish emulsion and set in an east window with sun for part of the day, or a few inches under the lights, the bulblets and plantlets will multiply and the mass of leaves spread to fill any size pot.

When your plant has grown overbig, you can break it up by simply cutting the mass of bulbs in sections and planting each part in a separate pot. Or the bulblets can be completely pulled apart. In that case, toss them into a plastic box with moist soil, cover them, keep them moist and, as they put up leaves, haul them out one by one and pot up. In that way you may, from a large plant, have over a hundred new ones.

Oxalis martiana grows in tropical America, and we always thought it was tender until a friend showed us a bed of them growing out of doors. A potful of bulblets had been emptied on an apartment-house flower bed in the city the previous fall. The pips had survived the winter and all had come up with plenty of leaves and flowers.

The plant will go dormant if you dry it out or subject it to coolness. But if you keep it constantly moist and warm, it will green and bloom continuously at all seasons. All oxalis is subject to mite attacks. If that happens spray with Kelthane solution three times, at intervals of a week. A lot of leaves will dry back, but new growth will soon replace them.

If you fail to keep the plant moist, it will go dormant. If attacked by mites and sprayed, it may not come back immediately. But it is not dead. Just take the whole pot, or the uprooted bulbs, and store them in the lower part of the refrigerator for a month. Then bring them out and water them. In a couple of weeks, new growth will appear.

The triangular leaf segments of Oxalis reg-nellii *are near to unique. Their undersides are burgundy red. This is the easiest of all the blooming houseplants to grow and virtually unkillable.*

The flowers of Pereskia aculeata. *They're yellow colored and lemon scented, but the "nose" is not its finest adornment.*

48 The Leafy Cactus
PERESKIA ACULEATA

Originally the world was a pretty watery place, and the land plants were similar to those that live today in the rain forests of the tropics. As more of the earth's surface dried out, whole families of plants disappeared, unable to adapt to the new circumstances. Some, which now inhabit the most arid regions, might have adapted themselves right where they were provided that the change took place very, very slowly. During the transition, plants would suffer severely and only those would remain alive that possessed some slightly superior ability to endure drought. As the dryness continued to increase, the characteristics of this desert group would become more and more different from the plants of the moister regions as they developed, painfully and infinitely slowly, the organs necessary for survival—fleshy bodies for water storage, a surface that permitted very little evaporation, deep roots, and very slow growth among other things.

There is also another way plants could have developed from moisture-loving to aridity-tolerant ones. Imagine a green region tapering off into a desert. Every year some seeds of plants from the moist areas would fall in drier zones. Of these only a few would survive over long periods and, after they had multiplied, would spread seed into still drier areas. Over millennia and even millions of years, stages of adaptation would move them farther and farther into the desert until they were suited to face the rigors of near total aridity. At the end of this development, the desert plants would no longer be recognizable, except to the eye of the botanist, as related to those they left behind them in moister regions.

Finally it is just possible that the primordial plants that had adapted themselves to the desert reversed the process and sent forth colonies to moister regions surrounding the deserts.

The cactus is a plant which is thought of so exclusively as an inhabitant of deserts in North and South America (there are no Old World cacti) that sections of the family that grow in the moist regions of the tropics are quite unfamiliar. Among these is the orchid cactus and cereus group, some of which climb trees of tropical forests and possess

115

The flower of Pereskia grandifolia *is cherry red and of the finest silk.*

the largest flowers in the family. If you see them, their cactus origin is not hard to recognize. Rhipsalis are more deceptive. They look often more like mistletoes than anything else. They have the round, often whitish, transparent berries and the same tubular stems. But there are also some with broad succulent leaves. Finally there are the pereskias, the least well known of these groups, and the only ones with leaves which are not truly succulent. Nevertheless they have the areoles and spines of cacti and are considered probably the most primitive of them all. Whether these are plants left behind in the forest when the cactus took to the desert or represent cactus adaptations to the moist tropics is hard to say. These too are vines but with normal-looking stems.

The most popular of the pereskias is *P. aculeata,* the lemon vine, which grows in the West Indies, has become naturalized in South Florida, and which also goes by the name of Barbados gooseberry. The fruits, it is said, are eaten raw and as a preserve, while the leaves are treated as potherbs. We have not tried them up to now, but you might like to experiment.

The vine grows rapidly and will soon reach the ceiling with the help of some support. We think of such plants as reaching for the light but they're not very logical about it. For instance, a recent example in our home grew up the length of the window but, instead of turning sideways to reach the maximum amount of light, kept going along the cornice until it got tired of being frustrated and just stopped growing. In the house it is always best to start trimming well before maximum height of windows is reached and keep on trimming, if it insists on branching at the tip, in order to induce more growth from below. Also, while the vine is growing so fast, the leaves stay small. It is only when they are stabilized that they reach maximum size.

The flowers—white, yellow, or pinkish—are about 1½ inches across with six to ten broad petals that overlap. They have a strong sweet lemon fragrance. The stigma protrudes on a long stalk from the center. And, as the flower, which remains on for a number of days, ages, the berry develops as the base of the stigma thickens into an odd dry brown

116

twisted protuberance. Eventually the petals fall off and the ⅜-inch yellow berry remains.

Pereskia can be grown at a window as a vine, trained in a circle on a pot trellis, or kept trimmed and grown under fluorescent lights. Give it Lean Mix with lime and treat altogether like a normal cactus except for higher temperatures—60° to 80° F—and somewhat more watering during the blooming season. In winter keep it quite dry and water just once a week lightly. Once a month, use fish emulsion in a dilution of one half that recommended on the label. The plant will bloom in partial shade.

Very floriferous and showy, this is one of the most interesting vines for the house. Flowering takes place in September-October and for the rest of the year the plant is either dormant or growing more stems and leaves.

A pereskia species (P. godseffiana) *with pure peached-colored leaves from Loyce's Gardens.*

The aluminum plant (Pilea cadieri). *Very common but, nevertheless, unique.*

49 The Aluminum Plant
PILEA CADIEREI

Ever since the male member of this team, at the tender age of six, fell into a ditch in a small village on a visit with his parents to Germany, he has known what a nettle is. The European stinging nettle is no fun, and you can be sure that George let out a howl that woke up the whole population napping in their armchairs that hot Sunday afternoon. Reddened skin on bare legs and arms announced the problem, and the cure was cooling compresses of water-soaked towels. No wonder he became a confirmed horticulturist.

It is difficult to believe that this tall repulsive weed with its drooping strands of tiny greenish flowers has numerous relatives which are of tropical origin and have been coming increasingly into favor as foliage houseplants. The reason is that the nettle family includes some small herbs with quite pretty leaves, which are nearly foolproof in cultivation. The flowers are tiny and usually tightly clustered. The genera *Pilea* and *Pellionia* are the chief contributors to horticulture. The pellionias mostly have brownish-zoned leaves and are flat trailing creepers. The pileas are more varied. Among them is the old and respected artillery plant and its relative the miniature artillery plant, notable for its tiny leaves—just weeds in the wild but amusing to some in the house. Personally we detest them. Then there is creeping Charlie, *Pilea nummularifolia,* and *P. depressa,* a totally undistinguished small-leaved plant useful for hanging baskets and pretty indestructible. *Pilea* 'Moon Valley' is the trademark name for an Asian species with quilted leaves—one of the more striking foliage plants but happier just received from the nursery than it is in your home—at least for most people. Additional species and hybrids zoned in brown and silver that have been introduced recently seem to have lost much of the vitality of the others and look better than they behave. What an extraordinary reper-

118

tory just the same for such an unpromising family! Here's a cheer for the nettles.

Although the name of the aluminum plant, *Pilea cadieri,* is generally known, the plants themselves are not offered by nurseries as frequently as one might expect. It is certainly the showiest of the pileas and absolutely easy to grow. Also it is unique among the foliage plants with its 2-inch-long leaves heavily quilted and zoned in pure aluminum against a green background. Aluminum is a good name, for the coloring is not silver as one might be tempted to believe. These leaves are borne on straight stiff fleshy stems, quite different from the other pileas. Under ideal conditions the plant will grow to 1½ feet but is easily kept 8 to 10 inches high by culture or by pruning.

Although it is tolerant of almost any kind of soil, we pot it in Rich Mix. We keep it constantly moist and feed it occasionally with balanced solutions. But its light requirement is remarkably low. We have had it in a northwest window between two walls of an apartment house and it did very well. Naturally the plant will look handsomer if the canes are strong and the leaves big and brilliant. And that comes with a little extra care. But maintenance is no problem at all.

It is also one of the easiest plants to propagate. Any piece of stem just stuck in the moist soil of the pot will root. An ideal beginner's plant and a genuine oddity.

The elegant flower of the yellow butterwort.

50 The Sly Butterwort
PINGUICULA LUTEA

Carnivorous plants are fascinating and suggestive. There are still stories circulating, believed by the credulous, that somewhere in the tropical forest world are man-eating plants, lianas no doubt, which creep up stealthily on snoozing explorers and gobble them down. Like so many other things written to satisfy the public desire for the irrational, this is pure poppycock. They probably originated as "tall stories," were repeated as a good conversational gambit, were "confirmed" somewhere along the line by a "scientist," and ended up in the receptive recording organs of the mindless. (Mindless people have been reported but not confirmed.)

The truth is strange enough. It is no fairy tale that a considerable number of plants have developed a taste for meat, and that, since they are too small to cope with beefsteak and sauce Béarnaise, manage very well with tiny insects. (Haven't people been known to eat chocolate-coated ants?) You might conceivably put this trait to use in the event of an invasion of gnats or fruit flies by laying in a supply of pinguiculas, droseras, sarracineas, and Venus-flytraps. We wouldn't be surprised if they took care of the situation.

Some of these meat eaters have a certain amount of mobility, such as Venus-flytraps, bladderworts, and sundews. But quite a lot just have vessels of one sort or another to which insects are attracted and from which they are unable to escape due to some ingenious structural arrangement. The pinguiculas, or butterworts, have the simplest setup.

120

Nothing violent about them—no watery dungeons, closing jaws, or sticky moving hairs enclosing the victim. And this is rather surprising considering that they are so closely related to the bladderworts which have the maddest and most complicated traps of all. (They are aquatic plants which actually suck in their prey. Whew.)

The butterwort's triangular or rounded, overlapping, fleshy, light green leaves form a succulent rosette on the ground. The surface of these leaves visibly perspires, but the sweat in this case consists of a sticky secretion that is attractive to small insects. Once these start feeding, they find their movements progressively more restricted by the goo which adheres to them. They may, for all we know, even be enjoying the sensation of gradually relaxing and going to sleep. But that means the end of them, and the secretion then proceeds to convert them into food for the plant. Neat.

The butterworts are particularly attractive as houseplants because of their small size and their charming, long-lasting flowers. The rosette of leaves never grows wider than about 3 inches and the single flowers are at the top of very thin 4-to-6-inch stalks. *P. lutea* is yellow but you may also come across the blue variety. The shape is that of a cornucopia balanced horizontally on a cradle—the calyx. The spur is very prominent and pert, the colors clear and rich. The yellow is deep, and the blue is dark and heavily veined. There aren't many comparably pretty flowers around.

Grow pinguiculas in a small-tank terrarium in sphagnum moss and sand or perlite. Keep the medium moist but without any excess liquid. Good reflected light from a window or about 8 inches under the fluorescent tubes is sufficient. Never place the terrarium in full sun. Pinguicula forms an excellent composition with sundews, Venus-flytraps, and small pitcher plants. In summer, a piece of fruit in the tank will attract fruit flies, which are excellent victims for these plants. Remember that they are not dependent on insects for nourishment. A very diluted watering with fish emulsion twice a year is advisable.

Platycerium alcicorne—*two stages.* Photo courtesy of Bernard
Alfieri.

51 The Staghorn Fern

PLATYCERIUM ALCICORNE (BIFURCATUM)

The staghorns are the most curious, the most different, and the most
aristocratic of ferns. A large specimen—2 or more feet across and 3 or 4
feet long—hanging on a wall in a living room, is so strange and exotic a
sight that it inevitably suggests expeditions to distant lands. It performs
much of the function of a moose or lion head in overawing a visitor. In
the game of plant one-upmanship, nothing works as well as a big
staghorn.

They are all tropical—from Australia, Africa, eastern Asia, and the
South Seas. Plenty of ferns perch in trees—usually along the boughs or
pockets in the trunk—as in some palms. But the staghorns plaster
themselves vertically onto trunks and, in spite of very little nutrition,
grow to an immense size. Old and huge examples can be seen in botanical gardens. On a large slab of wood or cork the sterile fronds,
almost round and very much like suction cups in appearance, are
stacked like the pages of a book. The ones nearer the slab are brown,
and the one or two on the very top have a fresh green velvetiness. The
fertile antlers grow out of the center, some broad and forked only at the
end, some narrow and split, depending on the species. Real granddad-
dies in good condition may consist of dozens of these ferns overlapping
each other and forming Niagaras of greenery.

The dead sterile fronds are a moisture-absorbent pad, which catches
water as it streams down the trunk of a tree. Debris, by its gradual
decomposition, nourishes the plant.

Staghorn ferns are very slow growing. With care a specimen may last
a generation. Few plants are less trouble to maintain.

Unless you are prepared to study ferns and learn how to handle
spores, it is not advisable to start with them. Small plants may be bought
in pots or attached to a support such as a slap of wood or cork bark. Size
of plant determines price which, nowadays, is by no means low.

The staghorn prefers a clay to a plastic pot. The reason is that the clay
absorbs moisture and is therefore damp on the outside. Mature ferns
drop their spores, which adhere to the outside of the pot and develop as

122

Young staghorn ferns in pot.

happily as if it were the trunk of a giant Australian forest tree. We have seen pots simply plastered with the young sterile frond pads. In time the pot disappears completely in the mass of fronds. You can grow the spores elsewhere, like seeds, but that takes a bit of expertise.

If you have bought a potted plant, place it in a north window or in soft reflected light. One of the great advantages is that, being used to growing well down on tree trunks, shaded by foliage, it manages with very little light. Place it at the ends or outside of your light garden. Soak the pot in lukewarm water thoroughly once a week. Fertilize once a month with a very weak solution of fish emulsion.

When the fern outgrows its pot, you do either of two things: if young'uns are attached already to the outside of the pot, clamp it to a board and hang it on a wall like a picture. Once a week take down your picture and give it its bath. Misting the leaves daily encourages growth.

When already attached to a board or cork by its own fine roots, just leave it that way. But if you wish to attach a young pot-grown plant to a board or cork, place a pad of osmunda or moss on the backing and wire the sterile frond into place. When it outgrows its board, just nail the smaller one to a larger one and the plant will spread and cover the unsightly joint.

Seedlings (really "sporelings") may be removed from a pot or the surface of a slab. Pot them up in a mixture of peat and sterilized gritty sand in equal proportions. If you want them on a separate board, attach them to a cushion of moss or osmunda and tie on with light wire. After a while, the leaf will hold onto the surface by itself and the binding can be removed.

Most staghorns prefer temperatures of 60° or higher. *P. alcicorne (bifurcatum)* is the one that can stand it down to 40°. Many others are adaptable to house temperatures. Pick out the pattern of leaf you like.

A collection of staghorn ferns in a greenhouse.

A big Polypodium aureum. *See the color illustration for the beautiful fur from which it grows.*

The Fur Blanket

52 POLYPODIUM AUREUM

If we were inventing names for a seed and plant catalog we would call *P. aureum* the Woolly Bear Fern. Somehow that suggests the extraordinary richness of the coloring and texture of its rhizomes better than the usual name, hare's foot fern.

Years ago we knew a lady who had a garden room with many plants of which the showpieces were two magnificent plants of this fern with leaves over four feet long. But it was the surface of the soil inside the tubs that really fascinated us, for the whole was blanketed with rich brown rhizomes. The hairs were almost as long and as thick and matted as the coat of an Airedale. There's a special kind of beauty attached to certain plant forms which suggest an explosion of vigor. Such are fat, luscious pseudobulbs of orchids. We felt the same way about the furry blanket of this fern but did not grow it for years for fear it would be too big to handle.

One day a friend gave us a young plant which already had a couple of 15-inch leaves. Cramped for space we worried about keeping it, but when challenged there is always room for one more plant. So we hung it in a window in a 10-inch clay azalea pot filled with Rich Mix and lime.

The plant grew up with astonishing speed, and soon there were a couple of dozen of the huge leaves making it quite a monumental production. The furry brown sausage of a rhizome with which our plant started soon had bumps of lighter color that slowly invaded the surrounding soil. As the growing tips increased in size, they changed in color from blonde to deep reddish tan, and the hairy surface became coarser and more woolly. Then, from another bump on its surface, the crozier of a new leaf would emerge and start to unroll. It was a fascinating operation to watch. The gradual expansion of a lead took several weeks. Sometimes a piece of rhizome emerged from the ground an inch or two away from the parent mass, grew larger and finally backspread to join with the rest. Sections grew out, curved, and curled back on themselves. In this seemingly haphazard way a solid blanket came into being. In some places it was quite smooth and low, and in others it humped an inch or more over the soil.

Eventually this fern became impossibly large, so we spoke to a florist nearby who offered to take it in. The following day we bore our huge creature through the streets. When we walked into the store, a gentleman was just leaving. He looked at the plant and inquired whether it needed much light. "Very little," I said, "it's a weed." "Is it for sale?" "That's up to Nanice; it's her plant." At that the gentleman called to the back of the store, "Nanice, I'll be back in fifteen minutes to negotiate." When Nanice saw the plant she said, "That isn't for sale. I'm taking it home." Of course we kept a piece of rhizome and root to start a new potful.

Polypodium aureum needs little attention. We fill the saucer once a week with water and fertilize it along with our other plants with whatever is being used at the moment. We suspect that it does not like overfeeding.

Our Fur Blanket comes from tropical America. East Asia is the source for other species with attractive rhizomes. Outstanding are the davallias—the squirrel's-foot and rabbit's-foot ferns. But these have hanging rhizomes that are quite different.

So perfect in color, texture, and form is the miniature jade tree that it seems artificial.

53 Miniature Jade Tree
PORTULACARIA AFRA-VARIEGATA

The object of bonsai is to train trees small to look like very old specimens of full-grown ones. Our miniature jade tree accomplishes this all by itself. With only the slightest encouragement, it looks like a greatly reduced granddaddy of a tree. The Chinese make little artificial trees of colored semiprecious stones. The fleshy little leaves of our tree are very similar. The Chinese also make figurines of ivory which they color in soft tints. Our tree's leaves, with their ivory, pink, and green coloration, and waxy substance, look as if they were made in the same way. We suppose a bonsai expert would want to prune and shape it. We, ourselves, love it as it is.

Portulacaria afra is green-leaved and grows to 12 feet in South Africa. The leaves are somewhat larger than our plant and the bloom is in tiny clusters. A visitor from South Africa was startled and fascinated by our little plant. Formerly the variegated form was rare, but lately commercial growers have recognized its superiority as a houseplant and sufficient plants are available.

Why is our plant so small? We suppose that it is a matter of chance culture. We started it in a 2-inch Japanese ceramic pot and there it has

The white, pink, and green waxy leaves of Portulacaria afra-variegata.

remained ever since, probably potbound. The results suggest just what you can do with this plant. Crowd its roots and nip the tip of the growth to promote branching and it will stay small and shapely.

Portulacaria is very, very slow growing in the house. I have had cuttings sitting for months with hardly any growth, but once it gets well rooted it branches beautifully and assumes a form that is classic in design.

Pot up a small specimen in Lean Mix with lime chips and pack very tightly. Keep slightly moist at all times as long as the temperature is over 60°. Below that, let the plant dry out and water only once a week.

Starting a cutting in the same medium, do not water at all at first. Merely spray every couple of days, so that there is some surface moisture absorbed by the soil.

Fertilizing tends to bring out coloring in leaves but should be carried on only once a month. We use fish emulsion. During hot days water more often but more lightly.

The variegation of this table fern is so feathery that it is one of the marvels of the plant world.

54 Variegated-Leaved Fern
PTERIS ENSIFORMIS CV. VICTORIAE

A little brake from eastern Asia is one of the most beautiful of foliage plants. Although variegation, the mixture of white with green in the leaves, is not unique with *Pteris ensiformis* cv. *Victoriae,* it is very special in its elegance of form and color. The infertile leaves are short and triangular with the leaflets split into rhombic sections, frilled at the edges, white along the midvein, and with some of the white penetrating into the green parts along the edges by means of the finest of brushings. The fertile fronds are narrow, long, and dull. So cut them off unless you want to collect spores.

A shade-loving plant in the outdoors, it can tolerate considerable shade in the home. Place it on the side of a window or at the end of a fluorescent lamp. Give it Rich Mix without lime and keep moist at all times and above 60° in winter. Temperatures above 85° cause suffering, and it requires high humidity. If you don't have a humidifier, take to the mister.

These cultural hints suggest that old *Victoriae* isn't quite that easy. In fact its great popularity is justified rather by its beauty than its perform- ance. Apparently it is very easy to propagate and grow into a 6-inch plant in a greenhouse, so that it makes a brave appearance on the shelves of a variety store where it is one of the favorite green plants with both seller and buyer. The trouble is that it is a well-behaved baby, but has a way of collapsing about the time it is ready to vote. Why this happens we do not know. Perhaps it's the heat of midsummer, a time when it usually occurs. We should think, therefore, that it will be hap- pier in an air-conditioned apartment. The plants are readily available so you can replace them easily, and one may come through in grand style for you.

We did have long-term success when it was planted in a corner of a fish tank terrarium. But it grew so big that we finally had to remove it—which ended its career as we had no larger container for it and exposure to normal humidity was fatal. But we do think that, if you have a good-sized, narrow terrarium which is rather high, you might put just one plant in it—the Victoria fern. Permitted to occupy all the space it will last a long time and display its striking foliage to best advantage.

The dwarf pomegranate in bloom. The pot is only a 2½-incher.

55 The Miracle Fruit Tree
PUNICA GRANATUM NANA

Fruit and flowers on a 6-inch-high tree in the middle of winter! Ridiculous—impossible—fake. What is this plant? Clue. It is associated with Persephone who was stolen from her mother Demeter and became the wife of Hades. When Zeus persuaded Hades to let her go, she visited the upper world but had to return eventually to the underworld because she had eaten seeds of this fruit. Finally a deal was arranged that Persephone would spend part of the year above and part of the year below ground. Clue. The Romans called it Punica because they thought it came from Carthage. Give up? Answer: dwarf pomegranate.

Full-sized pomegranates, which are as big as good-sized apples, grow on medium-sized trees. The leathery-skinned fruit with the rich red glow appears in our markets for a short time each fall. It is not easy to break the skin and once you've managed it you find that the interior is packed with seeds encased in juicy flesh. No wonder Persephone's travels represented the onset of winter and spring and that her pomegranate was a symbol of fertility. It's hard work eating this fruit, but children love them because they have the opportunity to squeeze each morsel and spit out the rest. If all the seeds grew we would be engulfed in pomegranate trees.

The dwarfing of the pomegranate must have taken place a long time ago because all around the Mediterranean they are grown as small shrubs and, like our indoor miniature, bear flaming flowers and little perfect reproductions of the larger fruit. The flowers have a tubular yellow calyx almost an inch long, whose surface is shiny as if it were lacquered. At the tip it breaks into five triangular lobes and out of the opening emerge the five crinkly silky petals, brilliantly red orange in color. Blow into the flower and it will usually set fruit. The calyx begins

The flower of the pomegranate is brilliant orange. Notice the unusual calyx.

to expand and soon looks like a little greenish yellow apple with a big tuft of the remains of the calyx sticking out in front. When it has reached a size of about 1½ inches in diameter it gradually turns more and more reddish and the skin hardens until it looks like the pomegranate it is. When the fruit is ripe, it can be removed from the tree, the skin opened, the seeds extracted and dried. You can have dozens of seedlings this way if you wish, but we find it easier to cut off branches and root them in moist vermiculite.

Pot up rooted cuttings with their little narrow oval leaves in Rich Mix with plenty of lime. Set the pot in a bright window or within 4 inches of the fluorescent tubes and keep moist at all times summer and winter. It likes a balanced fertilizer or fish emulsion with regular waterings. Temperature should be over 65° for flowers and best fruit development.

When the plant is 3 inches high it may start to bud. Considering that it is still weak, it is advisable to remove these first attempts and to prune the young stem so that it will produce plenty of branches. When it is 4 to 6 inches high, it can be allowed to bloom and set a fruit. However, the effort does exhaust the plant and flowering may be held up for quite some time. Only when you have a well-filled-out little tree 6 to 10 inches high is it advisable to encourage it to bear up to three fruits. The combination of continuous brilliant flowering and the showy fruits makes this the most wonderful of house plants. Flowering can be maintained all year round. No other shrubby houseplant matches this performance.

The ripening fruit of the dwarf pomegranate. The plant has been trained to a single stem.

We try to keep our plants in maximum 4-inch-diameter pots. It is a favorite of the new breed of indoor bonsai growers because it is so amenable to trimming and training. So let it be a challenge to keep your plant shapely and small. One of our friends trained it to have just two thick curving branches which she kept in fruit with the most decorative results imaginable. Sometimes we just train the tree with a straight trunk and a completely round mass of branches and leaves out of which flowers and fruit hang down. Such trees can live for a generation and never grow any further.

So here we have an indoor tree which is as odd and curious as you can wish, yet is a supremely good houseplant.

Rhipsalis houlletiana. *The small flowers line the leaves and are followed by berries.* Photo courtesy of Bernard Alfieri.

The white berries of Rhipsalis cassutha *are almost exactly like mistletoe. But you can't grow mistletoe indoors, while this plant is an easy one.*

56 False Mistletoe
RHIPSALIS SPECIES

Real Mistletoe, whatever kissing you do under it, goes by the formidable name of *Phoradendron flavescens* and is a noxious parasite on deciduous trees in our South as well as in Europe where the genus is *Viscum*. The Druids made a big thing of it and primitive peoples have attributed magical properties to it. It would be interesting to try to grow indoors with some tree offered as a sacrifice. But we don't know anyone who has tried it and suspect that it would succumb to domestication as do most parasitic plants. The distinguishing features are the naked stems, the thin leaves, and the white translucent and waxy berries.

The rhipsalis, which are epiphytic cacti, are very similar in growth but are not parasitic. Because their light demands are low and they need little attention, they do well in the house. Some of them have almost naked stems and others broad wavy dark green leaves which are usually narrow and long. The flowers with most species are rather inconspicuous and the chief ornaments are the clusters of white, yellowish, or pink berries. We cannot define the particular charm of this group but, whenever a fine collection is displayed—usually large plants in baskets—it arouses wonder and admiration. Perhaps it is their way of appearing as hazy masses of green, almost like artistic abstractions of plants, with delicate spots of color distributed here and there—the berries.

You may wonder what makes this very different plant a cactus. Well, all cacti, and no other plants, have hairy or soft spiny cushions called areoles on the leaves or along their edges. In the spiny cacti this is where the larger spines come out. Tropical cacti lack the spines. At the joints of

Rhipsalis or along the wavy edge of leaves, there are always areoles at intervals.

Rhipsalis comes in all sizes from such as mature at 6 or 8 inches to big basket plants that may stretch a yard or more across. There is tremendous variation in the shapes of leaves and stems. They grow much faster and easier than cacti, and you don't have to worry about overwatering or dormancy. They all root nicely in Rich Mix but will also take to any fibrous medium such as osmunda or mixtures of bark wool with perlite. Start with a 2½-inch pot and you will end up with a fine display plant if you choose.

When well-grown, the odd-shaped stems and leaves and colored berries complement modern furniture and decorations. Keep rhipsalis moist in reflected light and don't worry about them. Occasional sprayings are appreciated.

Some interesting species are *R. capilliformis, paradoxa, houlletiana, cereuscula,* and *pachyptera.* You have to see to believe them. The closely related *Hatiora salicornoides* has bottle-shaped joints for leaves and has gained the name of the Drunkard's Dream. It is particularly easy to grow but not as prolific or attractive as some of the true *Rhipsalis.*

Rhipsalis flowers can be charming though small. This close-up shows the very odd growth pattern. It's R. coriacea. Photo courtesy of Bernard Alfieri.

Pineapple sage, a pleasant plant with an extraordinary odor.

57 Pineapple Sage
SALVIA RUTILANS

You might think that herb enthusiasts would stick to growing plants which have a use. According to definition, a herb is a plant of value in cooking, in medicine, or as a fragrance in perfume. Happily they have extended their interests to those whose only attraction is their ability to imitate odors. We have already described the curry plant. Many of the fragrant geraniums are also grown only because they smell like lemon, mint, or rose. It is an odd hobby, for the fragrances do not permeate the air but are only apparent when they are stirred or the leaves are rubbed. One of the trickiest of these types of plants is the pineapple sage which has the advantage over some of the others of very pretty flowers.

The pineapple odor of the leaves when rubbed is a most extraordinary and unexpected counterfeit. With friends who do not know the plant it is surefire entertainment. That is true, however, only when it performs. We have had occasions when a guest was introduced to the plant with a suitable speech. Guest rubbed and sniffed but the olfactory organ recorded nothing. This leads to explanations and can be embarrassing. All we can say is that the plant does its thing most of the time (maybe company makes it shy) and that the pineapple odor is very intense. Contrary to some reports, laying a leaf or two in a gelatine dessert or the bottom of a cake pan provides neither pineapple flavor nor odor.

The leaves are pleasantly light green, pointy at both ends, and about 1½ inches long. In the house, allowed to take off, it will become a series of straggly, woody stems with a rosette of leaves at the ends. To prevent this you must nip the tip leaves when the plant is quite small in order to make it branch. Tipping is necessary, in fact, throughout its life if you want to have a bushy, good-looking plant.

Pineapple sage is not difficult to bring into bloom in spring and for that purpose can be allowed to grow freely for a while at that time. The blood red tube flowers are among the prettiest in the genus. Figure on an 8-inch or higher plant for flowering.

Grow *Salvia rutilans* in Rich Mix with lime and keep moist. The plant is a heavy drinker which, considering the thin leaves and woodiness, is surprising. It must perspire a lot. This is, by the way, not far from the truth. Lots of plants which are heavy drinkers are actually evaporating the moisture at a fast rate. Other plants that are faster growing and with thicker, juicier leaves and stems may have a slower rate of evaporation and need watering at longer intervals. Treat with balanced fertilizer. For light *Salvia rutilans* needs the brightest window but does well under fluorescent light with the top 4 inches below the lamps. Keep the temperature over 60° if you want good growth or bloom. A good size to maintain it is about 8 inches in all directions. Contrary to many of the herbs, *Salvia rutilans* winters well in the house.

The flowers of pineapple sage (Salvia rutilans) *are brilliant red.*

The strange flower of Sauromatum guttatum *grows directly from the bulb without planting or watering.* Photo courtesy of M. J. Martin, M.S.C., A.R.I.C.

The Largest Flower in the World And Its Smaller Edition for the House

 House

SAUROMATUM GUTTATUM, ETC.
(Amorphophallus titanum)
(Hydrosme rivieri)

The arums are a big family of plants growing in swampy places everywhere in the world. Jack-in-the-pulpit is a small-sized typical member. The striped pulpit with its canopy over Jack is a specialized leaf called a spathe, while Jack himself, a broomstick-shaped growth called a spadix, is the real flowering stalk covered with tiny blooms.

This will give you an idea of what *Amorphophallus titanum*, which is claimed to be the largest flower in the world, looks like. One of these bloomed at the New York Botanical Garden in 1937. The spathe was 4 feet broad and pointed straight upward. The top of the spadix was 8½ feet above its base. The tuber, which had been shipped from Sumatra in the East Indies, weighed in at 113½ pounds. Thousands who came to view this gigantic flower which, if filled with water, might well serve as a bathtub, kept a respectful distance. Whoever ventured close to it recoiled and took to flight pursued by its overpoweringly revolting stench.

Sauromatum's extraordinary single leaf. Photo courtesy of M. J. Martin, M.S.C., A.R.I.C.

One of the weird tropical arums, Hydrosme rivieri. *The flower is followed by a single magnificent leaf.* Photo courtesy of Thomas H. Everett.

If you want to bloom this plant in the house, nothing could be simpler. Just order a hundred pound dormant bulb from Sumatra, set it anywhere in a warm corner of the house, and in due time it will flower without any attention whatsoever. How you handle the problem of smell is up to you. You may be able to manage with a supply of deodorants.

Although we recognize the challenge to your ingenuity and fortitude involved in this situation, we guess that most people will be satisfied with growing one of this plant's still remarkable smaller relatives which are not at all forbidding.

One of the signs of spring is the appearance of numerous catalogs, listings, and advertisements in newspapers offering sensational plants, such as trees that bear five kinds of fruit. From the amount of space devoted to them at considerable cost it would seem that the attraction of a plant which is made to seem odd or curious is greater than a merely beautiful plant for the house. The choicest specimen of this appeal to public credulity is the devil's tongue or voodoo lily. Whatever the name invented by the dealer, the plants are actually either *Sauromatum guttatum* or *Hydrosme rivieri*, both from East Asia and much the same.

The accompanying picture shows a roundish bulb from which a colorful spathe grows to a grotesque height. The flower is described as gorgeous or spectacular. It ain't. It will also be claimed that the bulbs will bloom without being planted in soil. This is true. In fact, of all house plants, this is certainly the ultimate in foolproofing. However brown your thumb, your voodoo lily will perform.

The tubers are marketed at a time when they are about ready to pop—in March-April. Prices vary according to size of tuber, which ranges from 1½ to 4 inches in diameter, rarely more. Bring the tuber home and plunk it on a dish with the side up which has the point in the middle. Depending upon its mood, it may take anywhere from one to four weeks before it does anything. Then the flower pushes up rapidly, first as a furled smooth greenish point, then unfurling. It turns out to be some 6 to 10 inches tall and disappointingly dull.

When the flower wilts in a couple of weeks you come to the second, and for many the more attractive, stage. Pot the tuber in Rich Mix in a 6-inch pot. Plant it just below the surface of the soil, place it in a partially sunny window and fertilize with every watering. Use a 20–20–20 solution. Don't ever let it dry out from now on. Within a couple of weeks a single leaf will start to grow. It is a marvelous leaf on a long speckled stalk, spreading its segments to more than a foot across. It is very similar to but much bigger than that of green dragon, jack-in-the-pulpit's rarer wild native cousin. It provides handsome foliage and lasts for months. In the fall, when it dies down, stop watering entirely. Take out the tuber, allow it to dry and store it in a plastic bag until it starts to show a point the following spring.

Recently a dealer has been importing tubers of a species of *Amorphophallus.* They are of small size and will produce leaves only for the first couple of years. But, if you are patient, and have a large enough pot, it will eventually produce flowers which may reach a size of 12 inches across. However, such imports come and go and you will find any of the bulbs offered on the market about equally satisfactory. Most of the plants are either *Sauromatum guttatum* or *Hydrosme rivieri*—both from the East Asian regions.

During the summer the foliage likes misting occasionally. Winter temperature for the bulb should not go below 55°. Otherwise there is nothing to be concerned about with this easy plant.

The strawberry geranium's stolons with leaves have been pinned down in a little pot. Each will grow into a separate plant.

59 Strawberry Geranium
SAXIFRAGA SARMENTOSA (STOLONIFERA)

Our old and popular friend the strawberry geranium is neither a strawberry nor a geranium but looks a bit like a scented-leafed *Pelargonium* as to flower and has the runners of a strawberry. We include it here because of the latter. The instinct to motherhood is strong in this plant and population growth, were it not held in check by natural causes, would soon smother us all in its innumerable progeny.

Saxifraga sarmentosa, member of a family that produces many unusual and cherished Alpine flowers, comes from eastern Asia. Its low-growing leaves are rounded and turned down at the edge, lobed, and coarsely toothed. The dark green shiny surface is covered with a complex pattern of silver veinings while the underpart is pinkish. It blooms in spring with long spikes of airy little flowers having two long white petals below and three tiny pink ones above.

As soon as even a single cluster of leaves is well rooted, the strawberry geranium starts to send out wiry, nodeless stolons from the base. When we say nodeless, you understand of course that there is no interruption and that this suckering stem is as plain as a length of hose. This is indeed the nature of all stolons. The purpose is not to bear leaves, branches, and flowers but to act as a means of starting up business elsewhere. That is why the leaves are all clustered at the tip. You will notice that they are there even when the stolon is quite short and that they are carried farther and farther from the mother plant by its lengthening. When we root the tip we might compare it to establishing a branch store. And when we cut it free from the parent, it is like the manager of the store buying it and going into business for himself. Plantwise this gives us a number of possibilities for action.

Take a small plant of strawberry geranium and set it in the middle of an azalea pot. Pin down the ends of the stolons symmetrically around the mother plant and, in no time, you will have a beautifully arranged mass of foliage. Or set a ring of small pots with soil around the parent and fasten each stolon tip down with a hairpin. When they've rooted they can be separated from their mum. You can also hang the plant in the window and let the stolons and their clusters of leaves just trail.

Keep *Saxifraga sarmentosa* moist during the spring and summer months and a bit drier in winter. It prefers a bright spot at the window or under lights and a temperature of 65° or better. Use Lean Mix with lime and fertilize every couple of weeks with 20–20–20.

The variety 'Tricolor' is a showy, but ugly, combination of pink, white, and green leaves and is altogether more tender and difficult.

You may be interested to know that hydrangeas, currants, and gooseberries are also members of the saxifrage family.

60 Peacock Selaginella
SELAGINELLA UNCINATA
(See color section)

Selaginellas are very primitive plants which are botanically paired with the club mosses. They were among the earliest of the land plants and were widespread 300 million years ago at which time some were as tall as trees. Now they are common, ground-hugging plants of moist woods. Most people know the ground pines and shining club moss but selaginellas are not so obvious, though found in great numbers and variety in the tropics. They have tiny leaves on flat branches which have somewhat the appearance of miniature fern fronds.

These plants didn't interest us very much, though they have recently come into popularity for terrariums. Then, one day we were visiting the fern room of a botanical garden and, looking down on the moist, slimy soil, saw feathery growths that glinted with sharp points of iridescent blue. That grabbed us. An iridescent blue plant was worth considering. It looked insignificant from our height but we had learned that when small plants are seen indoors almost on a level with our eyes, they assume a quite different level of importance.

We noted the name of the plant—*Selaginella uncinata*—and soon acquired a starter plant whose progeny ever since have inhabited our terrariums. This feathery, lacy plant with its surprising color is a treasure every indoor gardener should grow.

In the steamy environment of a terrarium, selaginellas really go to town. Even a tiny piece soon takes hold in moist soil or moss and starts to reach for the light, putting out roots from various points on the branches. It can climb a foot into the air and still reach the soil with them and often they attach themselves to the glass and form a fascinating webbing on the moist surface. It has, in fact, all the characteristics of a banyan tree in miniature. If you don't like this undisciplined behavior all you have to do is push the mass of leaves down on the soil surface.

We find that all the selaginellas require a terrarium in the house and temperatures of 65° or better. *S. uncinata* doesn't always look blue. If it is unhappy and does not receive the correct amount of light, it will be just plain green. We find that it does well 15 to 18 inches under fluorescent tubes or in reflected light from a window. Usually it does not require fertilizer, but a very mild fish emulsion treatment once every three months does no harm.

When it is happy, selaginella will soon engulf other plants in a terrarium. But it is not difficult to keep it in check by removing excess branches, all of which can be started somewhere else. We've never had any pests or diseases on this plant.

141

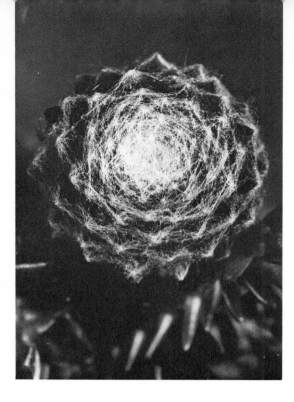

The cobweb houseleek in all its intricate glory.

61 The Spiderweb Plant
SEMPERVIVUM ARACHNOIDEUM

We don't have to introduce you to hen and chickens. It is the common *Sempervivum* which is one of the weediest of succulents, filling a pot in no time and trailing its rosettes down the side in its eagerness to produce. The species is called *tectorum* because, in Japan and East Asia, it pops up on the thatched roofs of the houses. Other favorite haunts are the crevices in large rocks, which it can cover for all their length in a single season. In late summer stout stems grow up from the center of the plant and for a short period there is a display of white, pink, or red star clusters.

There are many varieties of sempervivums growing in mountain regions and therefore rated OK for the hardy Alpine garden. The most curious of these in our eyes is *S. arachnoideum*, the spider-web or cobweb houseleek. It is a small plant, growing eventually 3 inches high on a thick stem and never more than about an inch across. The rosettes are tight leaved and rounded. From the tip of each leaf white hairs grow out symmetrically and overlap those from other leaves so that the whole top of the plant looks as if it were inhabited by a small, industrious spider that had used the leaf points as anchors for his webbing. The result is an elegant gossamer pattern that makes the other houseleeks look rather plebeian by comparison.

Although so small it is just as active as the other houseleeks in growing chicks. Only these develop not only from the base but often along the stem and crowd each other so that a well-developed colony several inches across is a bumpy mound of white fluff. In this condition it is no longer a cute little plant but quite handsome and noticeable. There are numerous variations at nurseries, and clumps of various sizes. It is up to you to pick out the prettiest ones. A sun-loving plant, it tolerates house conditions and grows normally in a bright window. You may even be able to achieve flowers—which grow on a stalk 6 inches high and are red.

Sempervivums flourish on most common soils, but like grit and gravel and some lime. So we give them Lean Mix with lime, set them in a sunny window and water regularly. Fish emulsion fertilizer four times a year is sufficient. If the light is inadequate, the plant will elongate and lose its compact habit, and offsets will be less numerous. They do perfectly well under fluorescent lights at a distance of about 8 inches. Temperature is not a factor in the house and high humidity is unnecessary. Without water they will shrivel, so don't mistake them for cacti.

The offsets are the usual source of new plants but seed germinates readily and can be treated like any other green-leaved plant in the early stages.

Green bead necklaces of Senecio rowleyanus.

62 The Bead Vine
SENECIO ROWLEYANUS

Because there is an element of surprise involved, the reactions of plant families to drastic environmental changes is always fascinating. For instance flowers of the two largest families respond very differently. Orchid flowers are the most variable of all, while those of the daisy family, to which the bead plant belongs, are all pretty much the same in appearance. Either they have rays or not. Those without are among the least attractive of all flowers. Except for details of structure, not apparent to laymen, the bead plant's flowers are hardly distinguishable from any number of common American weeds. It isn't for their sake that we admire *Senecio rowleyanus,* a South African succulent.

As similar as are daisy flowers, the habit of the plant can display great variety. *Senecio* is a big, worldwide genus among whose members are the florist cineraria, dusty miller, and the golden ragwort of our fields from Newfoundland to Florida. One marvels that the big triangular leaves of *Cineraria* or the much-dissected leaves of the ragwort should have evolved into such a simple form as a bead. There are plenty of near-succulent or succulent daisy plants which have developed needle-like leaves, but that is common to many families. What makes our oddity unique is the bead form which is matched by no other plant.

The "beads" of the common name—the leaves—have almost exactly the appearance of a rather widely spaced string of dark green, shiny jade beads. You could cut off a long strand, tie the ends behind your neck and go to a party, fooling everybody in sight. The smaller beads are almost round with just a hardly visible point at the tip. Larger ones are about ⅜ of an inch in diameter and somewhat persimmon shaped. Each bead has a narrow translucent line running vertically top to bottom. Whether or not this is one of those "windows" permitting light to filter down to a chlorophyll layer deep in the bead we do not know.

The round beads of rowleyanus *are not seeds but modified leaves.*

It's hard to believe that beady Senecio rowleyanus *can bloom but it does. The flowers are white, petalless daisies. The transparent line on the beads shows up well in this picture.*

When a bead vine had grown large in the house and hangs down on all sides of the pot, each bead separated by a fine green thread, the effect reminds us of those headdresses brides wear in the Orient, with strands of beads coming down half over the face. With careful arranging you can produce this pure fringe.

In spite of its odd form and contrary to many other desert-adapted

145

plants, *Senecio rowleyanus* is a fairly fast grower and very nearly foolproof.

If you start with seed, germination is quite rapid as with so many other daisies. Or you can buy a small pot of the growing vine. Hang in a window in anything from good reflected light to bright sun, or suspend from the shelf of your light unit and keep well watered. For this plant we find Lean Mix better than Cactus and Succulent Mix. As the strands lengthen, cut off pieces and pot them up separately. They'll root very quickly. Or tuck a piece of the length back into the soil of the pot and pin it down. Later, after rooting, you can cut it loose from the parent. In this way you can have one big or any number of small plants in short order.

The bead vine tolerates very dry atmosphere, any amount of heat, but doesn't like temperatures below 50° too well. If you have it in a cool room, water only when dry. Fertilize once a month with a balanced formula.

Formerly hard to come by, the bead vine has become popular recently and commercial nurseries have started to grow it in quantity. It is amazing how quickly these little plants disappear at a sale—proving that oddity does attract the indoor grower.

The elegant flower of tiny, everblooming Sinningia pusilla.

63 Little Marvel
SINNINGIA PUSILLA

For over a century the florist gloxinias, with funnel-shaped flowers, and the slipper gloxinias, both botanically sinningias, have been the big marvels among blooming houseplants. Producing quantities of very large flowers in a wide range of brilliant colors and blooming for several weeks in the house, they have enjoyed steady popularity. Nonetheless they were valued merely as gift plants. When they were done with flowering, most people just threw them out, not knowing that, if set aside for a few months, they would sprout and bloom again. The modern florist has objected to their very large leaves with brittle stems which make them difficult to ship.

Then along came, at the other end of the scale, that *little* marvel, *Sinningia pusilla*, which has meant more to indoor growers than any other plant except the African violet. It has gained popularity only recently, because it is so tiny that commercial growers rated it a poor investment. Consider that it forms a flat rosette no more than an inch across and that the flowers, on threadlike pedicels, are a lightish blue miniature of a slipper gloxinia only ½ inch long. It can be grown in a thimble or a plastic cream pot. There are two sports, both white, one of which has fringed petals. How small can a flowering plant be and still have any merit as a houseplant?

Well, *pusilla* has what it takes. Although it has a little tuber, about the size of a No. 1 sieve pea, and should go dormant, it doesn't. As soon as one growth has finished blooming, it's replaced by another. Seed is produced spontaneously and, unless you collect it religiously, the plant takes care of its own sowing. Soon the parent is ringed by a whole lot of baby pusillas all blooming like mad. An interesting feature of this charmer is that wherever it grows a very delicate moss starts up around it.

The miracle of everblooming gave hybridizers an idea. They started trying to cross *pusilla* with larger sinningias. It didn't work with the florist gloxinia but with a number of medium-size *Sinningia* species and with *Rechsteineria*, which is now also considered a sinningia. Another miniature, *Sinningia concinna*, more purplish and with purple dots in the throat, had similar characteristics but has proved more difficult to grow. This too was used for hybridizing. The result was a whole tribe of beautiful new houseplants, many of them everblooming, ranging in size from about double pusilla to plants with 1½- and 2-inch trumpet flowers. Some of these have become famous under names such as 'Dollbaby,' 'Cindy,' 'Pink Petite,' 'Little Imp,' and 'Big Imp,' 'Freckles,' 'Bright Eyes,' and 'Poupee.' These have been grown everywhere under fluorescent lights and provide flowering throughout the year. In most of this hybridizing, it was the tiny *pusilla* or *concinna* that was dominant and transferred its valuable characteristics to the offspring.

It is best to grow *S. pusilla* in a terrarium for it prefers high humidity, resents soggy medium, and requires very little light. In fact there are no other blooming plants we know of that need less. This means that in a terrarium *pusilla* can be placed low down in an arrangement or that the terrarium itself can be set at the end of the fluorescent tubes. The potting soil should be Rich Mix with lime, but *pusilla* will grow equally well on a bed of sphagnum or other mosses. Maintain a temperature of 65° or higher. We fertilize not at all.

Three conditions will make *S. pusilla* go dormant—coolness, drying it out, and overwatering. If the top growth should die off, remember there is a small tuber beneath the soil surface and that the plant is never dead until the tuber rots.

Get acquainted with this little marvel and use it in terrariums, around other plants and in tiny pots of its own. You will never tire of it and discover that this is one of the most extraordinary plants of all.

The huge bud of Stapelia gigantea.

64 The Giant Carrion Flower
STAPELIA GIGANTEA

It is hard to believe that some plants of the milkweed family are related, so extraordinary are the differences between them. As we've pointed out, though (p. 48), those fluffy seeds are always much the same. There is also another trick that identifies them no matter what the disguise. This is that the pollen masses are hung from a tiny slit structure within the flower. Bees, butterflies, or flies that land on it to feed catch their legs in this clip and have to haul out the whole business or lose a leg. Watch Monarch butterflies or bees feeding on the common milkweed. In a few minutes you will notice that at least one of them has gone completely berserk. With its leg stuck in the flower it flies around and around, trying to escape. We've been astonished at how long a bee's leg is once it's stretched out. The struggle may last quite a long time and usually succeeds, for it is no advantage to the flower to gain a leg and not have its pollen transported to another flower.

In spite of appearances stapelias and their relatives are all legitimate members of the milkweed family. Long ago they had regular leaves and probably made a good living in India. Then, because of the pressure of population or some climate change perhaps, they started to migrate. In doing so they usually invaded very dry regions and, in the process, lost

their leaves and became columnar plants like some cacti and euphorbias. Like an invading army, they moved first to northern Africa and
Arabia and then gradually worked their way south. The largest divisions
were held up finally by the Cape of Good Hope, a region which they
must have found to their liking, for they there produced their most
spectacular species and the greatest number of varieties.

The stapelia columns are spineless but often very bumpy. They stand
up straight along the ground, connected at the base by thick stems, and
never or rarely branch, remaining much the same height. So far they are
no different in appearance from many other desert plants. The flowers
are the shocker—and you'll never believe they are real. Imagine a
star-shaped flower covered with inch-long hairs, or one covered with
tiny, pen-and-ink lines, or striped like a zebra, or the center having a
raised ring like the planet Saturn. If this boggles your imagination—go
look at a flower; it's all there.

Let's face it, stapelias stink. They are fertilized by flies and have
apparently discovered that the most agreeable and attractive odor is, as
one might expect, rotten meat. People make an awful fuss about that.
But, when you come right down to the realities, we suspect that they are
really showing off their stinky blooms. For the smell doesn't reach very
far and nobody obliges you to stick your nose into the flower. We don't
sniff at odorless flowers, so why go out of your way to test the perfume
of this one? The important thing is that the plant is relatively small and
neat and the flowers are relatively large and totally original.

Among the stapelias is one named *Stapelia gigantea,* and another
called *Stapelia nobilis,* which is very similar though a bit smaller. These
two have four-angled velvety stems about 6 inches tall and crawl along

The bud splits.

The first petal about to spring up. Notice how it pulls the tip of the bud around.

the ground spreading into quite handsome columnar clusters. But the bud and flower are where the action is.

The bud develops on a short pedicel at the base of the stem. It grows and grows until it is a tremendous pointed turnip-shaped balloon made of segments of dull tan silk sewn together. One morning it starts to open up—usually around 11 A.M. Figuring that the performance will be on schedule we often invite several friends over to see the event. All of a sudden a triangular section works itself loose, trailing long hairs along its edges, and literally pops open. Then there's a pause of several minutes while you try to peak into the innards. Pop goes another segment. Then a long wait and still another. At the end of the act, which may take an hour, an open star, 11 inches across, lies half on the ground or tray, half against its column. The star has a rubbled yellow background marked with short concentric lines of deep red. It is just unbelievable that the squat stem could have produced a flower of this size—larger than any of our garden flowers except a giant dahlia.

The flower lasts only a couple of days but, on a well-grown plant, many buds appear, and the show can go on for weeks. It is an easy plant to grow in the house and bloom is almost certain—provided you have a bright windowsill or fluorescent lights. With the lights you even get bloom at odd times throughout the year—to the envy of your windowsill growing friends.

Pot stapelias in Lean Mix with a top dressing of gravel. This is very necessary because they can take a lot of watering at times, but will suddenly and mysteriously start to rot if they are in contact with moisture during any sudden drop of temperature, or very humid conditions in summer. Fertilize only once every month with a mild solution of fish emulsion. Good reflected light or direct sunlight will suit it equally well. Under fluorescent light it thrives 6 inches below the tubes. *S. gigantea* is rather big for a light garden, primarily because of its spreading habit. Needing very little soil for its roots, it crawls right out of a pot and keeps

151

The fully extended petal.

going. Two- and 3-foot-long plants are not uncommon. When buds appear cut out watering until flowering is over and let the plant dry a bit for a couple of weeks thereafter. The compost can be kept moderately moist most of the time.

To propagate just cut off a stem, allow it to dry out for two or three days, then plant in moist Lean Mix. Thereafter allow the soil to dry out completely and spray just enough so that there is some rundown. When growth resumes you can start to water regularly.

If *S. gigantea* is too big for you, the smaller, but equally remarkable *S. variegata* and *S. hirsuta* will do as well or better. Both of these bloom more often than *S. gigantea.* And what a show. *Variegata* has a star-shaped flower 3 inches across with a wonderful doughnut-shaped ring in the center (an annular ring) and odd markings in deep cordovan red on dull yellow with an almost iridescent greenish tinge. *Hirsuta* is an odd purplish red covered with inch-long white or greyish hairs so thickly packed that they look like true fur. The flower is 5 inches in diameter. There are many fascinating related plants—huernias, duvalias, caral-lumas—that are now readily available from succulent nurseries and that supply an endless variation of forms in the stems and designs and colors in the flowers.

A most fascinating small garden could be made of a mixed collection of South African succulents, keeping in mind the paintings of Picasso and Yves Tanguy. Both painted canvases that contain science-fiction Mars-style figures emerging from sandy wastes. Combine stapelias with living stones, succulent euphorbias, fenestrarias, etc. Add a few bleached bones and some colorful jewellike real stones—preferably polished. If this is done imaginatively, you will have a living surrealistic picture and put Dali to shame.

The incredible 11-inch flower of Stapelia gigantea.

Stapelia variegata—*small plant, big flower. That's the annular ring in the center of the flower.*

Tillandsia ionantha in bloom. It gets a succession of deep purple flowers tipped with yellow. The leaves turn brilliant red. The white fuzz is made up of scales that absorb moisture and nutriment from the air on which this extraordinary plant largely depends. The span is about 2½ inches.

65 The Blushing Air Plant
TILLANDSIA IONANTHA

Like cacti the bromeliads are entirely New World plants. The cactus family is so varied that it is very special, but other parts of the world have similar desert plants. The bromeliads, however, are unique, since their roots serve almost exclusively for attachment and they have had to develop unusual ways of nourishing themselves. One of these is to produce broad curved leaves, overlapping to form a container in which water collects. Others have leaves coated with minute scales that absorb moisture from the air. It is the second kind that comes by its nickname of air plant rightfully.

Most of the real air plants belong to the genus *Tillandsia.* They are still quite common in Florida. Spanish moss, which drapes the trees, and ball moss, which perches happily on electric and telephone wires, can't be missed. It is a marvel that they exist, grow, flower, and produce seed on so Spartan a diet. Other tillandsias are often strange twisted ampule-shaped plants, parched grey in color. They attach themselves to the trunks and limbs of trees. Two, *T. cyanea* and *T. lindenii,* produce quite large three-petaled blue flowers and make excellent houseplants. But our favorite is little *Tillandsia ionantha,* which is exquisite and easy to grow.

It is a little fountain of narrow straight or curving grey leaves that look quite dead until they are moistened, whereupon they turn a soft green for a short time. Individually the plants are usually no more than a couple of inches across and high, often growing in thick clumps. This characteristic is the joy of some bromeliad fanciers who make a moss cylinder or use a tree fern pole to which they attach plants at regular intervals. These, spreading with time, eventually cover it with thousands of progeny.

154

Tillandsia recurvata, *ball moss, a close relative of* T. ionantha *and Spanish moss. In the South, Spanish moss decorates the trees and ball moss finds a happy roost on telephone wires and twigs. The little flowers are purple. If it did not require very high humidity and lots of air circulation, this would be a fun plant for the house.*

For most of the year ionanthas just grow very slowly and compensate by their smallness for not being decorative. But when they have once decided to bloom, usually in winter or early spring, all the leaves turn within a week or two a flaming red, and out of the center emerge, one by one, inch-long deep purple tube flowers topped by a fuzzy yellow cluster of anthers. This display, considering the small size, is sensational. It lasts several weeks. Then the color gradually fades and the plant prepares for its final act. It produces suckers at the base and proceeds to die. The suckers are the young plants, which can be left to grow where they are or be separated and potted up.

T. ionantha is usually shipped out of pot, so the first thing you have to do is give it a roost. If you want it to grow symmetrically, it is best to fill a little pot with osmunda or any other fibrous organic material, poke a bit of a hole and fit the bottom of the plant into it. If it is unsteady, you may have to tie it down. After a few weeks it will support itself. This is the best procedure in the house because bromeliads depend on very high humidity and tropical rains in their habitat. It is easier to keep them moist in a pot.

The other way is to attach the plant to a piece of cork bark, driftwood, tree fern, or the like. A length of fine wire looped around its base will hold it tight. Or gouge a small hole in the dry material, drop a bit of Elmer's glue into it, and if the plant is supported for a few minutes it'll adhere.

Place your plant in a south window or close under the fluorescent lamps and spray daily. If the spray contains just a smidgen of fish emulsion, it will be appreciated. Although it likes a daily moistening, ionantha does not want to be wet for long.

If you like ionantha try some of the other wonderful colorful bromeliads. They come in all sizes and some are among the most decorative of our foliage plants. The most incredible flowering we have ever seen was of an immense *Bromelia balansae* whose 6-foot, ferociously spiny leaves turned as violently red as *ionantha* and from the center a 4-or-5-inch thick column rose that was solidly packed with purple flowers and ivory bracts. Breathtaking is the word. Easy to grow, compact, and colorful are the earth stars or *Cryptanthus* species. Needing little attention yet so rewarding as decoration you should be growing more kinds of bromeliads.

SOURCES OF SUPPLIES

AQUATIC PLANTS

Slocum Water Gardens, 1101 Cypress Gardens Rd., Winter Haven, Florida 33880. Catalog 25¢.

Three Springs Fisheries, Lilypons, Maryland 21717. Catalog 50¢.

William Tricker, 174 Allendale Avenue, Saddle River, New Jersey 07458. Catalog.

Van Ness Water Gardens, 2460 N. Euclid Avenue, Upland, California 71986. Catalog 25¢.

BROMELIADS

Alberts & Merkel Bros., Boynton Beach, Florida 33435.

Bennett's Bromeliads, Box 1532, Winter Park, Florida 32789. List for 10¢ stamp.

Cornelison Bromeliads, 225 San Bernardino, North Fort Myers, Florida 33903. List for 10¢ stamp.

Seaborn Del Dios Nursery, R. 3, Box 455, Escondido, California 92025. List.

Velco Importers, 4212 W. Jefferson Blvd., Los Angeles, California 90016.

CACTI AND SUCCULENTS

Abbey Garden, 176 Toro Canyon Road, Carpinteria, California 93013.

Cactus by Mueller, 10411 Rosedale Hwy., Bakersfield, California 91308.

Cactus Gem Nursery, Box 327, Aromas, California 95004.

Desert Nursery, 21595 Box Springs Road, Riverside, California 92507. Aloes.

Desert Plant Co., Box 880, Marfa, Texas 79843.

Grigsby Cactus Gardens, 2326 Bella Vista Dr., Vista, California 92083.

Henrietta's Nursery, 1345 N. Brawley, Fresno, California 93705.

Singer's Growing Things, 6385 Enfield Avenue, Reseda, California 91335.

Ed Storms, 4223 Pershing, Fort Worth, Texas 76107. Lithops and other succulents.

CARNIVOROUS PLANTS

Peter Paul's Nurseries, Darcy Road, Canandaigua, New York 14424.

Plant Oddities, Box 127, Basking Ridge, New Jersey 07920.

Sun Dew Environments, P.O. Box 503, Boston, Massachusetts 02115.

Harold Welsh, 266 Kipp Street, Hackensack, New Jersey 07601.

GESNERIADS

Buell's, Box 218, Eastford, Connecticut 06242. Famous for gloxinias and other gesneriads. List 25¢ plus stamped, self-addressed envelope.

L. Easterbrook Greenhouses, 10 Craig Street, Butler, Ohio 44822. Huge list 50¢.

Fischer Greenhouses, Linwood, New Jersey 08221. African violets.

Kartuz Greenhouses, Wilmington, Massachusetts 01884. Gesneriads and begonias. Many novelties. List 50¢.

Lauray of Salisbury, Under Mountain Road, Salisbury, Connecticut 06068. Gesneriads, succulents, and numerous houseplants. List 50¢.

Lyndon Lyon, Dolgeville, New York 13329. African violets and other gesneriads. List 10¢.

Tinari Greenhouses, 2325 Valley Road, Huntingdon Valley, Pennsylvania 19006. Gesneriads and light gardening supplies. List 25¢.

Whistling Hill, Box 27, Hamburg, New York 14075. Gesneriads. Many species. List 25¢.

HERBS

Caprilands Herb Farm, Coventry, Connecticut 06238. Plants and seeds. Lists.

Carroll Gardens, Westminster, Maryland 21157. Catalog.

Green Herb Gardens, Greene, Rhode Island 02827. List.

Hemlock Hill Herb Farm, Litchfield, Connecticut 06759.

Logee's Greenhouse, 55 North Street, Danielson, Connecticut. Catalog $1.00.

Merry Gardens, Camden, Maine 04843. Catalog $1.00. List 25¢.

Sunnybrook Herb Farm, Chesterfield, Ohio 44026. Catalog 25¢.

HOUSE PLANT SUPPLIES AND EQUIPMENT

Flora Greenhouses, Box 1191,

Burlingame, California 94010. Fluorescent fixtures.

Floralite Company, 4124 E. Oakwood Rd., Oak Creek, Wisconsin 53154. Fluorescent plant stands.

The Green House, 9515 Flower Street, Bellflower, California 90706. Fluorescent units.

Vernard J. Greeson, 3548 N. Cramer St., Milwaukee, Wisconsin 53211. Houseplant supplies and equipment. List 10¢.

The House Plant Corner, Box 5000, Cambridge, Maryland 21613. Extensive catalog of supplies and equipment including fluorescent fixtures.

Lifelite Incorporated, 1025 Shary Circle, Concord, California 94520. Fluorescent equipment.

Norran Inc., 14957 Lakewood Heights Boulevard, Cleveland, Ohio 44107. Fluorescent units.

Paragon Time Control, Inc., Three Rivers, Wisconsin. Timers.

Geo. W. Park Seed Co., Inc., Greenwood, South Carolina 29646. Supplies.

The Plant Room, 6373 Trafalgar Road, Hornby, Ontario, Canada. Full line of supplies.

Al Saffer & Co., Inc., 130 West 28th Street, New York, New York 10001. Extensive catalog of equipment and supplies.

Shoplite Co., 566 Franklin Avenue, Nutley, New Jersey 07110. Fluorescent equipment. Catalog 25¢.

Tropical Plant Products, Inc., P.O.B. 7754, Orlando, Florida 32804. Orchid media, fertilizers, indoor gardening supplies.

Fred A. Veith, 3505 Mozart Avenue, Cincinnati, Ohio 45211. Houseplant supplies.

ORCHIDS

Alberts & Merkel Bros., Boynton

Beach, Florida 33435. Great collection of orchids and other tropical plants. List.

Haussermann Orchids, Box 353, Elmhurst, Illinois 60126. Catalog.

Jones & Scully, 2200 N.W. 33rd Avenue, Miami, Florida 33142. Catalog.

Rod McLellan Co., 1450 El Camino Real, South San Francisco, California 94080. Catalog.

Fred A. Stewart, 1212 E. Las Tunas Dr., San Gabriel, California 91778. Catalog $1.00.

SEED

Most plant societies have seed funds from which members may purchase by mail. Listings are usually included in their publications.

John Brudy's Rare Plant House, Box 84, Cocoa Beach, Florida 32931. List.

W. Atlee Burpee, Philadelphia, Pennsylvania 19132; Clinton, Iowa 52732; Riverside, California 92504. Catalog.

De Sylva Seeds, 29114 Tanager Street, Colton, California 92324. List.

Deedee's, Box 416, Menlo Park, California 94025. List.

J. L. Hudson Seedsman, Box 1058, Redwood City, California 94064. Catalog 50¢.

Le Jardin du Gourmet, Box 119, Ramsey, New Jersey 07446. Carries French herb seeds.

Mail Box Seeds, 2042 Encinal Avenue, Alameda, California 9501.

New Mexico Cactus Research, Box 787, Belen, New Mexico 87002. Extensive list of cacti and succulents.

Nichols Garden Nursery, 1190 N. Pacific Hwy., Albany, Oregon 97321. Catalog.

Geo. W. Park Seed Co., Greenwood, South Carolina 29646.

Stokes Seeds, Box 548, Buffalo, New York 14240.

SEMPERVIVUMS, ETC.

Arcady Gardens, 2646 Calhoun Road, Medford, Oregon 97501. List.

Palette Gardens, 26 W. Zion Hills Road, Quakertown, Pennsylvania 18951. Sempervivums and Alpine plants. List.

TROPICAL HOUSE PLANTS

Alberts & Merkel Bros., Boynton Beach, Florida 33435.

Farm & Garden Nursery, 116 Reade Street, New York, New York 10013.

International Growers Exchange, P.O.B. 397, Farmington, Michigan 48024.

Lauray of Salisbury, Under Mountain Road, Salisbury, Connecticut 06068.

Loyce's Flowers, R.2, Box 11, Granbury, Texas 76048. Hoyas, hibiscus, bougainvillaeas. List 25¢.

McComb's Greenhouses, New Straitsville, Ohio 43766.

Merry Gardens, Camden, Maine 04843.

Norvell Greenhouses, 318 S. Greenacres Road, Greenacres, Washington 99016. Catalog 25¢.

Novel Plants, Bridgeton, Indiana 47836. List 10¢.

Geo. W. Park Seed Co., Greenwood, South Carolina 29646. Catalog.

Plant Oddities, Box 127, Basking Ridge, New Jersey 07920. Carnivorous plants. Catalog 25¢.

The Plant Room, 6373 Trafalgar Road, Hornby, Ontario, Canada.

Tropical Gardens, R.R. 1, Box 143, Greenwood, Indiana 46142.

Tropical Paradise Greenhouse, 8825 W. 79th Street, Overland Park, Kansas 66104.

Williford's Nursery, Rte. 3, Smithfield, North Carolina 27577. Catalog 25¢.

Wyrtzen Exotic Plants, 165 Bryant Avenue, Floral Park, New York 11001. Begonias and gesneriads. List.

PLANT SOCIETIES

American Begonia Society,
Ms. Betty Burrell,
14050 Ramona Dr.,
Whittier, California 90605.
Annual dues: $4.00. Monthly
Publication: *The Begonian.*
Seed Fund.

American Bonsai Society,
Herbert R. Brawner,
229 North Shore Dr.,
Lake Waukomis,
Parkville, Missouri 64151.
Annual dues: $10.00.
Quarterly publication:
The Bonsai Journal.

American Fern Society,
Dept. of Botany, Univ. of Rhode
Island,
Kingston, Rhode Island 02881.
Annual dues: $5.00.
Quarterly publication: *American
Fern Journal.*

American Gesneriad Society,
Edmund O. Sherer,
11983 Darlington Avenue,
Los Angeles, California 90049.
Annual dues: $5.25.
Bimonthly magazine.

American Gloxinia & Gesneriad
Society,
Mrs. J. W. Rowe,
Box 174, New Milford,
Connecticut 06776.
Annual dues: $5.00. Seed Fund.

American Orchid Society,
Botanical Museum of Harvard
University,

Cambridge, Massachusetts 02138.
Annual dues: $12.50. Monthly
publication.

Bromeliad Society,
Membership Secretary,
Box 3279, Santa Monica,
California 90403.
Annual dues: $7.50.
Bimonthly journal.

Cactus and Succulent Society of
America,
Box 187, Reseda, California
91335.
Annual dues: $7.50. Bimonthly
publication: *The Cactus and
Succulent Journal.*

Epiphyllum Society of America,
218 E. Greystone Avenue,
Monrovia, California 91016.
Annual dues: $2.00. Publication
7 times a year of *Epiphyllum
Bulletin.*

Indoor Light Garden Society of
America, Inc.,
Mrs. James Martin,
423 Powell Drive,
Bay Village, Ohio 44140.
Annual dues: $5.00. Bimonthly
publication: *Light Garden.*
Seed Fund. Chapters.

Saintpaulia International,
Box 459, Knoxville, Tennessee
37901.
Annual dues: $5.25. Bimonthly
publication: *Gesneriad-Saint-
paulia News.*

INDEX

c.1

635.9 Elbert, Virginie F.
E
    Fun with growing odd
    and curious house
    plants

DATE		
DE 4 '86		
DE 16 '86		
JA 6 '87		
JA 20 '87		

© THE BAKER & TAYLOR CO.